UNDERSTANDING

SHOWMANSHIP

Everything You Need to Know
to Win in Showmanship Classes

LAURIE TRUSKAUSKAS

Alpine
PUBLICATIONS
Loveland, Colorado

Understanding Showmanship
Copyright © 2001 Laurie Truskauskas

Library of Congress Cataloging-in-Publication Data

Truskauskas, Laurie, 1957
Understanding Showmanship : everything you need to know to win in showmanship classes
/ Laurie Truskauskas ;
      p. cm
ISBN 1-57779-030-8
1. Horses--showing. 2. Horse shows. I. Title

SF294.5. T78 2000
636.1'0811--dc21   00-063967

This book is available at special quantity discounts for club promotions, premiums, or educational use. Write for details.

The information contained in this book is complete and accurate to the best of our knowledge. All recommendations are made without guarantee on the part of the author or Alpine Publications, Inc. The author and publisher disclaim any liability with the use of this information.

Designed by: Laura Claassen
Photos: Dave Hamrick (unless otherwise noted)
Illustrations: Elizabeth Marshall

First printing: May 2001

1 2 3 4 5 6 7 8 9 0

Printed in the United States of America.

CONTENTS

DEDICATION

This book is dedicated to all the horses I've trained (and their owners)
that teach me just a little more every day of my life;
and to all the people in Texas, especially in the Athens area, who have
made my move here so rewarding. Thank you!

ACKNOWLEDGMENTS

To Traci Phillips, whose six-year-old chestnut and white Paint overo stallion, Dee's Lucky Charmer, one of the stallions that stand at my Silver Creek Farm in Athens, Texas, for stud service. Another is a jet black Quarter Horse stallion, Dangerous Devil Dan, and the third is SC Splashs Robinboy, a black and white Paint stallion. Not only does Dee's Lucky Charmer—alias Studly—pass on his color and wonderful, easygoing disposition to his colts, he performs the showmanship maneuvers with ease. Good ground manners are especially important in breeding stallions, and we took it one step farther and taught him showmanship. He possesses that eye-catching, winning look and special charisma that shouts, "Look at me! Aren't I grand?" Traci volunteered her stallion and herself to model for some of the photos in this book as long as we shot the pictures before her first pregnancy became too obvious. Thanks, Traci!

To Evelyn McKinney, who loves the Showmanship Class and has gathered many AQHA points with various horses. It was her idea that this book should be written. That thought was confirmed by an equine bookstore owner at the 1998 Quarter Horse Congress, who said that she receives many calls for a book on showmanship but that none are available on the subject. One is sorely needed, especially as this class gains in popularity. Evelyn read the last draft of this book and gave me a few helpful tips to add to various chapters that I might have otherwise missed. She also volunteered to model for pictures for this book.

To Jackie Tomlinson, who helped do the button braids, and to Teresa Grubbs, owner of Teddy's Principle—alias Teddy—who modeled the button braids.

To all the other horses (and their owners) that I use for models for various books and articles.

To all of the clients at my farm who help when the days get long and time gets short.

To Betty McKinney and the staff at Alpine for putting these pages into book form and being understanding when I submitted this manuscript a few days late.

To my kids and grandson, who still love me, even though I'm far away.

And to my mother, who helps me every day.

FOREWORD

TO THE PURCHASERS OF THIS BOOK: I commend you on your choice. You have made an invaluable purchase that will help you for many years to come. This book will be a valuable reference in your equine library with its systematic approach to learning.

To Laurie, I thank you for taking your valuable time to write this book so that the rest of us may read and learn from your enormous wealth of knowledge and experience. You have the enviable ability to simplify in words tasks that are sometimes very complicated.

This book, in its straightforward manner, is written with the novice in mind, yet does not forget those who participate at the bigger breed shows and seek to improve their skills. It will develop your expertise, educate you and encourage you to participate in an event that you may have felt is only for the most experienced of horsemen and women. Following this step-by-step approach, even the greenest novice can soon be showing competitively.

And for moms and dads of a "wannabe" youth exhibitor, here is your answer —help with the basics of showmanship.

Evelyn McKinney
Member AQHA, APHA, PBHA

Presentation is the key to showmanship.

CHAPTER ONE

WHAT IS SHOWMANSHIP?

SHOWMANSHIP IS THE ART of showing a horse at halter. The horse himself is not judged. The horse is merely a prop that you use to demonstrate your ability to show a horse to his best advantage. You are judged on your ability to fit or to properly condition a horse as well as on your ability to present yourself professionally and properly and to show the horse as you would a halter horse. *You* are judged on the neatness of your attire, the cleanliness of your tack, and the execution of your pattern.

Although you are being judged, not your horse, you are being judged on *your ability to show a horse*. Therefore, the *horse* is where you should aim most of your attention. You must be aware, at all times, of where the judge is located in relation to you and your horse. Yet, first and foremost, you must be sure that your horse is standing correctly and has not cocked a leg, moved "out of square," or done

In a showmanship class, the handlers are judged on how well they present their horse at halter.

Be aware of where the judge is at all times.

any number of other things that an enterprising horse may try to do to break up the monotony of the class. If your only reason for showing in this class is to show off your new outfit or your new figure, find a beauty pageant. If you want to participate in showmanship and show a horse, you must learn to be aware at all times of where the judge is and of what your horse is doing. You want your horse to look his best at all times. Over-presenting yourself is a large turnoff to many judges. The American Quarter Horse Association (AQHA) rules specifically state: "The exhibitor should appear businesslike, stand and move in a straight, natural, and upright manner, and avoid excessive, unnatural, or animated body positions."

Showmanship originated as a way to teach a handler how to best show a horse at halter. In a halter class, the horses are divided by age and sex, and the horse himself is judged. In a halter class, you show the *horse*. Your handling ability is not judged. Yet, the way in which you present your horse can add or detract from the appearance of the horse and therefore affect the horse's final placement. For that reason, it is wise to study the mechanics of showing at showmanship to understand how to better show your horse at halter, even if you choose never to show in a showmanship class. However, showmanship is a fun class that can be mastered easily. It is easier to train a horse to lead and set up correctly than it is to teach him to perform a reining pattern, jump a course of eight fences, or move slowly yet correctly in a western pleasure class. Another benefit of showmanship is that you do not need to own a superior halter horse or a top moving hunter or pleasure horse to place well. You must, however, do your homework and teach your horse to move correctly on the ground and to be obedient to your every body movement and cue in order to place in a top-level showmanship class.

Showmanship is often the first class in which a new competitor will begin to do well, and doing well in one class gives you the incentive to try other classes. Showmanship is the class in which I began winning consistently as a child, and those ribbons gave me the incentive to keep trying until I began to place in other riding classes. (My very *first* ribbon was in a musical chairs class—a fifth place, green rosette.)

THE ART OF SHOWING A HORSE

As I mentioned earlier, showmanship is an art. You must be proud of your horse to show him, because that attitude will be evident in how you present your horse. Dragging the horse along behind you tells a judge that you have not done your homework and taught your horse to lead correctly, nor do you care enough about placing in this class to spend the time learning and training your horse to be competitive. You cannot pull a horse out of the pasture on a Saturday night and expect him to do well at showmanship on Sunday. You

The difference is obvious in a horse prepared for showmanship as compared to a horse pulled out of the pasture.

must teach him to lead and to back up, to set up, to perform the 360 (planting his hind pivot foot in the ground), and to hold his square position as you move back and forth in front of him. I use the "quarter method" of showing, which will be described in Chapter 7.

TRAINING

Training a horse to perform the maneuvers required in a showmanship class does not require as large a commitment of time as do some of the other more demanding classes. However, your showmanship horse must be clean and conditioned, and he must obey your slightest command by barely a whisper of a lead-line cue. After a period of time, if a horse is trained consistently, he *will* learn to interpret your body language as his cue to perform. At that point, you should be able to put in a competitive round in a showmanship class.

CONFORMATION

While your showmanship horse does not need to have the conformation of a superior halter horse, at the higher levels of showing, a nicely

An out-of-condition horse.

What a difference sixty days made!

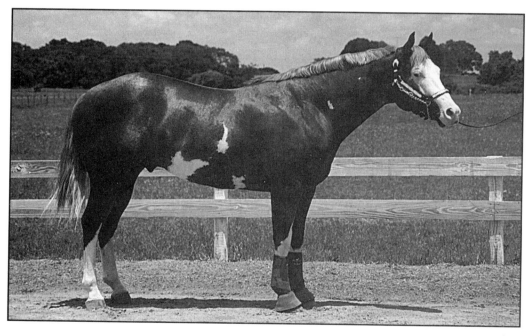

conformed horse with an eye-catching presence will often make the difference between a first and second place. That is not to say that you can't beat the more nicely built horse, because you certainly can if you put in your time and train your horse well. But if two handlers are equal in their showmanship performance, many times the ribbon will go to the more eye-catching horse that shows charisma. If your goal is to buy a new showmanship horse, keep that thought in mind.

CONDITIONING

Conditioning plays a large part in the appearance of your horse, and it shows that you care enough about your horse and about your placing in this class to do well. A well-conditioned horse always looks better than an overweight, out-of-condition horse. Conditioning does not happen overnight. It must be done right so as not to stress your horse and cause him to become sore or lame. Working an overweight horse too hard, too soon, can cause him to pull a muscle, bow a tendon, become colicky, tie up, or endure many other complications that can be avoided simply by building him up to good condition *slowly* and thoughtfully. In thirty days you will see your horse begin to improve, and you just keep building on that.

Conditioning takes time and effort on your part. Not only will your well-conditioned horse do better or place higher in his showmanship class, he will feel better, look better, and stay healthier. Even if a showmanship class is not in your near future, conditioning should be part of your horse's normal routine if only to keep him healthy. A horse is not much different than a person who works in an office all week, sitting at a desk, then tries to jog ten miles or play three games of tennis on the weekend. He will be sore from overexertion because his body is not properly conditioned to handle the demands placed on his muscles. Along the same line, if you let an out-of-condition horse out to play in a pasture or paddock, he is more prone to sustaining strains and pulls because of his lack of fitness. Conditioning makes good sense for both horse and handler.

A young horse can be lightly conditioned, but be careful that young, growing bones and tendons are not stressed. Some problems that occur at a young age are irreversible. A young horse that is fed too much to make him grow faster can develop osteochondrosis dessicans (OCD), which occurs when bone growth is too fast and too soft to accommodate the tendon and muscle mass. The lower bones of the legs bow forward because of the pull on the back of the tendon.

TEACHING SHOWMANSHIP MANEUVERS

Teaching your horse the showmanship maneuvers makes sense not only for showmanship class, but for safety reasons as well. Learning to lead, stand, and obey your requests from the ground teaches a horse to be mannerly, obedient, and *safe.* Showmanship maneuvers, the quarter method in particular, came into being to promote safety when working with a thousand-plus-pound animal controlled by only a small strap of leather.

The object of showmanship is for you, the handler, to learn to move in such a manner that the judge always has a clear, unobstructed view of your horse. When he is at the left front of the horse, you will stand on the right front of the horse. Standing in that position allows him an unobstructed view of the horse and allows you to pull your horse's head away from the judge if your horse tries to nip or bite him. When the judge progresses to the hindquarters, you move to the same side of the horse as the judge, yet you do not block his view because, even though you face the horse, you stand to the side and slightly to the front of him. The reason for moving to this position is, again, for safety. If you need to, you can pull the horse's head toward you and his hindquarters will swing harmlessly away from the judge.

Learning to be respectful on the ground also helps a horse to be respectful under saddle. Good ground training and proper manners will do much toward having a safe and obedient horse to handle, both on the ground and when you are on his back. A horse that thinks he is a playmate is not safe or fun for anyone to work with. Teach your horse good ground manners right from the start and you will be well on your way to teaching the showmanship maneuvers.

Your horse must be obedient to the whoa command, which helps with ground work and when you ride. Your horse must learn to obey your requests without question so that you both can enjoy a long and successful relationship whenever and wherever you work around him.

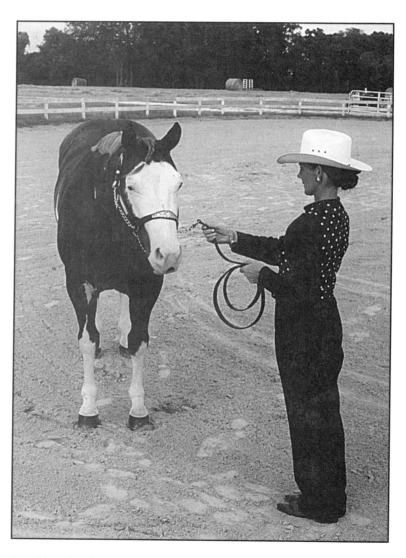

Teaching the showmanship maneuvers produces a well-mannered horse. (The author with Studly.)

CHAPTER TWO

VOCABULARY

THE VOCABULARY, or the terms that you will see listed for your showmanship pattern, is really quite simple. After all, there are only so many things that a judge can ask you to do with a horse on the end of a lead line. But you must remember to read and learn to understand exactly what the judge is asking for with the pattern he chooses so that you may perform it precisely as it is written. Your maneuvers should appear effortless and seamless—in other words, one maneuver should blend in with the maneuver that follows. Points will be taken off your score if you add maneuvers or do not perform the maneuvers exactly as they are written. The more precision there is in your pattern, the higher you will score. A poorly done pattern does not show the accuracy and dazzle of a more polished pattern that will win a class. Anyone can learn to perform a showmanship pattern, but it takes time and practice to show a *perfect* pattern with a fit and clean horse that is beside you every step of the way.

Let's look at some of the terms that you might see, and learn what the judge expects with the words he has chosen to explain his pattern to you.

Walk to the first cone: While the pattern won't normally say (in words) which side of the cone on which to start, the drawing that accompanies the pattern should show you. If you start on the left, have your horse on the left side of the cone. Don't make your first step until your horse makes a step. Walk

Lead your horse in a straight line. Stay at his throat latch.

7

briskly without looking at your horse. He should be beside you every step of the way. If the pattern calls for a trot at the second cone, start trotting precisely when your horse's front leg *is at the cone*. Precision is a must!

Leading. Always lead a horse from the left side and stay at his throat latch, slightly away from him so that if he moves his head or even spooks he won't bump you. You must leave him a little room to maneuver so that he can track in a straight line at both the walk and trot. Loop the balance of your lead rope in large loops. Never tightly coil the balance of the lead line around your hand because you could get dragged if your horse were to spook. Do not fold the excess lead line. The rules state that it must be coiled in large loops. Hold your right hand on the leather strap, not on the chain segment of the lead line, and keep your hand level with the halter. Carry the balance of the lead line looped in your left hand, held no lower than your waist.

Stop with your horse's front feet at the cone. Give the judge an unobstructed view.

Trot to the second cone. Teach your horse to obey a non-verbal (body language) signal to trot—and allow him to trot alongside you. Don't drag him, get in front of him, or allow him to drag you. Do not begin to make trotting steps until your horse begins to trot. Be sure that you travel in a straight line to the next cone, or to the next maneuver, unless that pattern specifically calls for a curved line. Again, don't look at your horse—he should be right beside you.

Back up. When a judge calls for a certain number of steps backward, be sure to back up *exactly* the number of steps that the pattern calls for. If the pattern says to back up to the cone, then back up as many steps as are required.

When you stop to ask your horse to back up, he should stop with his feet squarely underneath him—that is your goal in training. Now, turn and face your horse. To begin the turn, take a step with your left foot, pivot to face the horse, then bring your right foot to meet your left foot. You are now facing the horse with your feet aimed at his hind end. To have your horse back up, walk forward, facing your horse's rump, as he walks backward. Your right arm (with the lead line in that hand) crosses your chest, and you hold the lead line under your horse's chin.

Ninety-degree turn. A ninety-degree turn is a one-quarter turn to the right. When you are asked to do a ninety-degree turn, you your-self do a quarter-turn first so that you face your horse. Then step into the horse and push him to the right, asking him to make the quarter turn. His left front leg should cross over *in front of*—not behind—the right front leg. Walk briskly so that the horse steps around the turn with impulsion. Do not ask the horse to back into the turn, and do not use your lead line to force him to back up even slightly. That would cause him to cross his left front leg in back of the right front leg.

180-degree turn. A 180-degree turn is a half-turn to the right. When you do a 180-degree turn, you ask the horse to turn back in the direction from which he just came. The same rules as for the ninety-degree turn apply, but you make a half-turn rather than a quarter-turn.

270-degree turn. A 270-degree turn is three-quarters of a turn. The same rules apply as for the ninety-degree turn.

360-degree turn. A 360-degree turn is a full turn in place with the horse pivoting on his right hind foot while his body remains straight from head to tail. The same rules

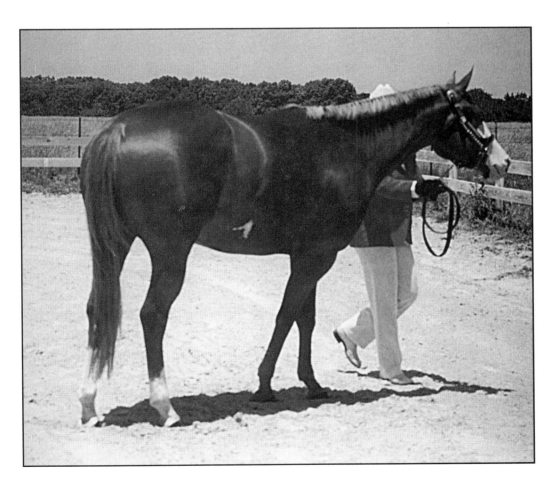

The mare's body remains aligned from head to tail as she pivots around her right hind foot, always crossing her left front foot in front of the right front foot. Photo by Cayla McKinney.

She remains straight throughout the turn, crossing over in front.

In this photo, the handler switches hands on the lead rope to create more impulsion. (This is acceptable for training, but not for showing). Photo by Cayla McKinney.

apply as for the ninety-degree turn. Remember that when you walk the 360-degree turn, *you* should walk a perfect circle, because that will help the horse to keep his form and to pivot on his right hind foot, rather than walk forward out of the turn or back out of a correct 360 due to incorrect forward or backward pressure on the lead line.

horse to set up. While the judge may not say a word, he will mark you down for taking longer than three seconds.

Your horse should set up with a minimum of cues from you and should hold that square position until you tell him otherwise. Teaching the set-up is discussed in Chapter 7.

Set up. When you set up your Quarter Horse, Paint horse, or other stock-horse breed, make sure that his four legs are set squarely underneath him. Practice at home so that you learn exactly where his legs should be positioned so that he does not appear camped out or set too close (looking like a circus horse perched on a stool). You have three seconds or less to ask the

Return to lineup. Unless stated otherwise, any time a pattern calls for you to come out of the lineup to perform a pattern, and then to return to the lineup, you will go back through the line of other horses at whatever gait your return to the lineup calls for. (The lineup area is designated by the ring steward as you enter the arena and is where the horses are positioned side by side

1) Execution of the 90-, 180-, and the 360-degree turns all involve the same principle: start with your horse square.

2) To begin, first turn and face your horse. Step with your right foot at the same time as you extend your right hand to cue the horse to pivot (or perform the turn). Be sure to keep your shoulders square and your body aligned from head to toe.

3) You can see this horse planting his right hind pivot foot as he begins to make the turn.

4) Be sure to leave yourself enough room so that you don't knock over the cone as you make the turn.

5) Ready for inspection upon completion of the turn.

waiting their turn to perform.) Once you are through the line of horses, stop, do a 180-degree turn, walk your horse back to the lineup, and set up. Do not get too close to the horses on either side of you, and try not to distract them as you set up once again in the lineup.

While the vocabulary of a showmanship class is quite easy, knowing what the judge expects of each maneuver and then putting it together with the one that follows in a seamless presentation will gain you the highest points on the pattern segment of the class. Ask questions, practice at home, work on the maneuvers on which your horse needs to practice, and be sure to read your pattern and follow it exactly as written!

Always give the judge an unobstructed view of the horse. The tape on the horse shows the quarters discussed in Chapter 7.

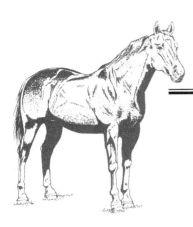

CHAPTER THREE

THE HANDLER

YOUR FIRST SHOWMANSHIP CLASS is right around the corner. Your horse is groomed to perfection, knows the maneuvers forward and backward, and is conditioned and sparkling clean. But what about you? What do you need to know? Before you walk into your first and succeeding classes, be sure that your attitude is right. You must enter the ring expecting to win. That does not mean that you become angry or upset if you do not win, because good sportsmanship is a must! You may face this same judge on a different day at a different show, and judges seldom forget a poor sport. Your attitude must convey to the judge that you know you have the best horse, that you have done your homework, and that you expect to win because of your superior ability to show a horse.

The first minute or two of your entrance into the ring tells a judge more than you might imagine. If you are alert, cheerful, bright, and smiling, without being fake or overdone, that tells the judge that you are prepared to show your horse to his best ability and that

Put on a happy face. Smile! This is fun!

Present your horse to the best of your ability so that you make an attractive picture to the judge.

you know you can win this class. Of course, only one handler gets the blue ribbon, but that one person *can* be you, and you must let the judge know that is exactly what you think—that you deserve the blue ribbon. If you drag your horse behind you, if your horse will not trot when you ask him to, and if he will not set up in a few seconds, the judge will see that you have not done your homework and therefore you do not expect to win this class.

PRACTICE, PRACTICE, PRACTICE

While it is probably easier to train a showmanship horse to perform the maneuvers required of him than it is to teach him to jump, rein, or perform western pleasure, you cannot drag a horse out of the pasture and expect to win. You must spend the time at home teaching your horse to obey your barely seen lead-line cues that tell him to set up, to trot when asked, or to

perform the 360. You must practice these maneuvers. You cannot expect your horse to do well because he is pretty or knows how to lead. There is much more to this class than a horse that leads alongside you. However, if you spend ten to fifteen minutes per day for sixty to ninety days, your horse should learn the skills he needs to do well at this class. This class is easy to master in respect to time invested when compared to many of the riding classes.

SHOWMANSHIP IS A PICTURE

If you think of showmanship as a way to present a horse to a prospective buyer, it will help you to portray the image you must present to win. You also sell yourself as the best person to market the horse. Showmanship is presentation. Your presentation of this horse can make a prospective buyer want to own this horse, or you can turn him off to the sale forever. Everyone wants a well-behaved, mannerly horse—a horse that leads alongside you attentively, that stops and squares up as soon as you ask him to, and one that stands quietly as you show him. Good ground manners give the image of a horse that has been handled; therefore, most people would assume that this horse has been trained and is one that they would want to own. Looking at a horse that prances and dances, or fidgets or kicks, would not make you want to own this horse. Good ground manners show a horse's ability to be handled easily. Teaching a horse to respect you on the ground will help teach him to respect you once you are on his back. Respect from the ground *does* carry over to work on a horse's back. For that reason alone, teaching a horse proper ground manners is a good idea. You can teach showmanship maneuvers to a young horse that is not old enough to be ridden. Ground training will help you when the time comes to saddle break and ride him.

KNOW THE PATTERN

Before you enter the arena to perform your showmanship patterns, be sure that you know and understand the pattern completely. Everyone has their own way of memorizing a pattern. I can give you tips on methods that have worked for some of my students, but ultimately, you must find the method that works for you. For some, writing the pattern will help them to remember it. For example, on a piece of paper, write out in longhand, "Walk to the first cone. Set up. Perform a 360-turn in place. Trot to the judge, back five steps, then make a ninety-degree turn to

the right and proceed to the line-up."

Other people will need to see where the cones are placed as they repeat the directions to themselves. Some will walk the pattern, turning in place without the horse, then jogging a few steps before turning to the right and walking a few more steps to the imaginary lineup. Others will take their horse through the entire pattern. Still others will need to watch a few horses go through the pattern to get it set in their mind.

You could be asked to go first, however, so you must know the pattern. Going first can be to your benefit—if you know the pattern. You will set the standard that others must follow.

PLAN AHEAD

When you first see a pattern, run through it in your mind. For example, if you must perform a 360 *by or before* a cone, you must stop before your horse's nose reaches the cone, allowing the horse to make the turn and return to where he started the 360. If you are asked to perform a 360 *at* a cone, then you must leave a horse length (left to right) between your horse and the cone so that the horse can make the complete 360-degree turn without ending up on top of the cone. If you stop with your horse's head right by the cone, he will knock the cone over when he finishes his turn. This is a severe fault. (Be sure to look at the pattern to see which way the judge wants to see you perform it, or ask before you start if you are unclear about the directions.)

If you must make a ninety-degree turn and then walk to the judge, plan your turn so that you

Illustrations of sample patterns. From easy to...

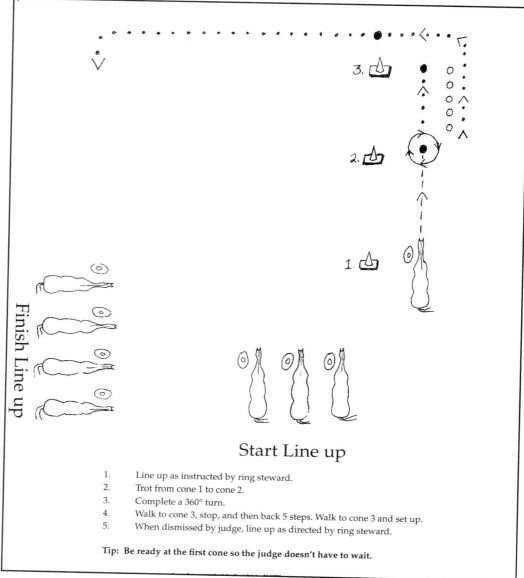

Finish Line up

Start Line up

1.   Line up as instructed by ring steward.
2.   Trot from cone 1 to cone 2.
3.   Complete a 360° turn.
4.   Walk to cone 3, stop, and then back 5 steps. Walk to cone 3 and set up.
5.   When dismissed by judge, line up as directed by ring steward.

Tip: Be ready at the first cone so the judge doesn't have to wait.

will be lined up directly with the judge after you make the quarter turn. In this case, your horse's *hip* should be lined up with the judge so that when you pivot the horse, his head will be in line with the judge. Then you can track in a straight line to the judge.

Think ahead! Think of how you can best show off your horse's ability. Your lines and patterns must always be straight. Pick a point directly in front of where you are going and learn to walk straight to that point. Pick a point that is

high enough so that you can keep your head up and look proud of the horse that you are showing.

The rules have changed over the years. It is no longer acceptable to look back at your horse every few seconds to be sure that he is right alongside you. You must trust your horse to follow where you lead while you look at the judge. This is where your homework pays off. You can look at your horse at home to be sure that he is correct. A show is a report card of all that you have taught him at home.

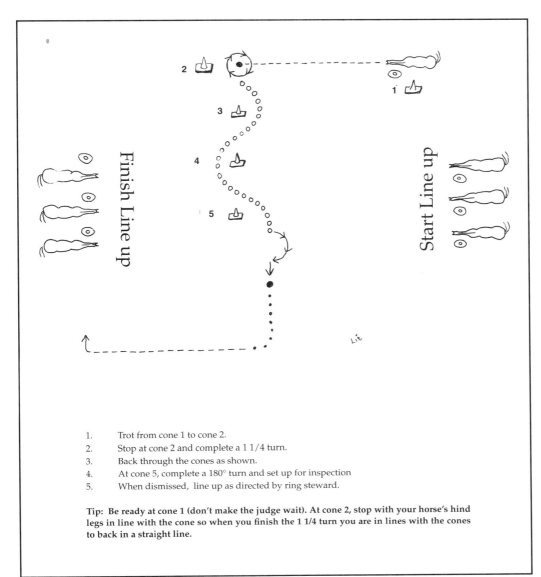

...hard—or a more advanced pattern. The variety is endless. Practice the maneuvers so that you can put each maneuver into a seamless pattern as called for at a show.

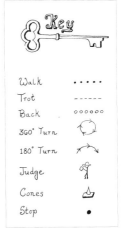

1.   Trot from cone 1 to cone 2.
2.   Stop at cone 2 and complete a 1 1/4 turn.
3.   Back through the cones as shown.
4.   At cone 5, complete a 180° turn and set up for inspection
5.   When dismissed, line up as directed by ring steward.

Tip: Be ready at cone 1 (don't make the judge wait). At cone 2, stop with your horse's hind legs in line with the cone so when you finish the 1 1/4 turn you are in lines with the cones to back in a straight line.

GIVE THE JUDGE AN UNOBSTRUCTED VIEW

Carefully read the chapter on the quarter method of showing. I have used masking tape to section my model horse into quarters. When the judge is in one quarter at the right front of the horse, you must be at the left front of the horse. This is for safety reasons. If your horse tries to bite or nip the judge, you can pull his head toward you. While you won't gain points for preventing such an ordeal, you will surely lose points if you allow your horse to bite. *Never anticipate* the judge moving from one quarter to the next; he leads and you follow, just as if you are dancing with a partner. You must let the judge lead this dance. A nicely presented showmanship pattern looks similar to a graceful dance. That is your goal.

Once you have practiced the showmanship maneuvers, memorized your pattern, and you know and understand where you must stand in relation to the judge, you are well on your way to developing

A nicely dressed exhibitor with a well-presented horse with that eye-catching charisma. Both horse and handler shout, "Look at me!" A winning team!

a winning pattern. If you enter the ring with a clean, fit horse that is attractive and has that certain charisma which says "look at me!", if your halter and lead line are clean and shining and your own appearance says that you are serious about winning, you'll be on your way to gathering those showmanship points.

CHAPTER FOUR

THE SHOWMANSHIP PROSPECT

IF YOU ARE LOOKING for a showmanship prospect as a first horse, or to replace an existing horse with a more competitive showmanship horse, here are some guidelines that may help in your search. The three most important qualities are a good disposition and quiet temperament; a horse that is eye-catching, balanced, and well put together; and a horse which compliments the handler's size.

GOOD DISPOSITION

Look for a horse that is not easily ruffled by the commotion, noises, and distractions of a horse-show setting. Most horses eventually will learn to accept the distractions of a show, but that can take time. The horse will need to be exposed to different settings——indoor and outdoor arenas, commotion, and other animals. Choosing a quiet, well-mannered horse shortens the length of time it takes to get a horse show-ready.

If you are buying a youth horse, then calmness becomes even more of a factor. A spooky horse always presents a slight element of danger before he learns that "horsey monsters" do not live at horse shows. I have taken retired racehorses to their first show and spent three to four hours walking them, without ever entering a class, are then loading up to go home. Racehorses are exposed to so much that you would expect them to take this in stride, I have found the opposite to be true. Whether they assume that a show is a race day, or the first show just makes them nervous, I don't know.

However, you are always better off to attend a show or two and just let your horse walk around the grounds. Do not enter any classes until the horse settles down and adjusts to this new setting. While much of this time-consuming training can be avoided by having a quiet horse, a first show for any horse should be entered with the thought of gaining ring experience, not with the purpose of winning.

Generally speaking, a quiet horse learns easier and retains his knowledge better, if only because he can keep his mind on the job at hand. (One cannot teach a horse any specialized work, such as reining, jumping or trail, until he becomes quiet under saddle.)

Choose a horse that already has good ground manners and one that leads well. While many training problems can be fixed with time, patience, and a consistent training program, unless the horse is a steal of a buy and has the other qualities necessary, it is best to continue your search until you find a horse that already has good manners. Otherwise, you must be willing to spend time re-training basic ground manners before you can start working on the showmanship maneuvers.

EYE APPEAL

The second important quality for a showmanship horse is eye appeal. Although the showmanship class is based on a *handler's ability* to show a horse, a prettier or more eye-catching horse might sway a judge in your favor. The judge's first impression of an eye-catching, well-presented horse is that of a winner. Of course you have to make that horse look as sharp as possible: He must be well-conditioned with a shiny hair coat and a sparkling, tangle-free mane and tail. A better handler can beat you with a lesser-quality horse, but, if everything else is equal, a horse with more eye appeal may give you that slight edge.

What constitutes eye appeal? A pretty head, a long, slender neck, and a well-proportioned body—a look of overall balance. Other eye catchers are a good hair coat, sparkling clean tack that fits well, attractive clothes on the handler that match the horse, and a neatly banded mane. A horse with four matching socks, although they're harder to keep clean, will set him

apart from his solid-legged cousins. (It's called "chrome.") A pretty-headed horse with overall balance and a healthy, gleaming hair coat shouts, "Look at me! Aren't I pretty?"

Some horses have a certain charisma or presence. These horses carry themselves as if they *know* they're gorgeous. Some horses, like some people, want to show off to a crowd. If this horse's energy or presence is dedicated to performing his showmanship job, he'll be hard to beat if you do *your* part correctly.

MATCH YOUR HORSE'S SIZE TO YOUR OWN

While some people might think it cute to see a little girl leading a big, stout mare or gelding, from a judge's point of view it is better to match the size of the horse to the handler. Again, you are looking for that balanced picture. If you buy a youth horse for your child, then you probably will have to buy a larger horse when your child grows and start the showmanship training all over again.

The good news about showmanship is that within ninety days of consistent training a horse is normally ready to attend his first show. You might have to use the first few shows to gain ring experience rather than going to win, but showmanship is one of the easier classes to train for.

Because showmanship is judged on the handler and how that handler fits and presents the horse, a horse with minor conformation faults will place over a so-called "better" horse—a horse with better conformation. Eye appeal is a nice, finishing touch, but the real

Betrayed Lady, a Thoroughbred mare owned by Rick Bourland.

test is how well you fit and present the horse. A well-conditioned horse always looks better than a fat, out-of-shape horse, so plan on putting some time into getting even the best horse into show condition.

No specific type of horse is required for showmanship; however, look for a horse with eye appeal as demonstrated in the following photographs.

Sally (palomino mare), owned by Terry Carter.

Dee's Lucky Charmer (alias Studly), a Paint stallion) owned by Traci Phillips.

Sidonie, a Paint yearling owned by Aaron Boswell.

Big Red, Thoroughbred gelding owned by Rick Bourland.

Sunny, a palomino gelding owned by Terry Carter.

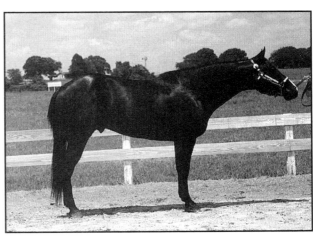

Dangerous Devil Dan, Quarter Horse stallion owned by John Morris.

SC Splashsrobinboy, Paint stallion owned by the author, Laurie Truskauskas, and standing at Silver Creek Farm, Athens, Texas.

Dusty, Quarter Horse gelding owned by Jacki Stutzman.

Queenie (Quarter Horse mare) owned by Gary Walsh.

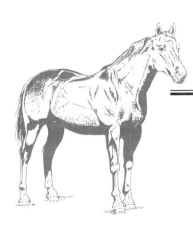

CHAPTER FIVE

CLOTHES AND ACCESSORIES

THE CLOTHES THAT YOU WEAR should put the polish on an already professional picture. Your clothes should compliment the color of your horse as well as your skin tone and hair color. Choose colors that you are comfortable wearing. Clothes that are comfortable in color, fit, and style will help you feel good about yourself. If you wear a style or color that is not you, you'll feel self-conscious and will lose that winning charisma.

While judge-length jackets are currently in style for the bigger shows, a vest that matches your shirt and pants can change the look of your outfit for a smaller show. You can create several different outfits by changing your shirt or vest or the color of your pants, without the expense of a second jacket. If you show every weekend, you will want several different outfits for variety. Black may be a prominent color in a pleasure or riding class, but black doesn't work well in a showmanship class. Colored jackets, vests, or shirts with embroidery on the front are currently popular. Crystals that pick up light are also popular in showmanship but are

more appropriate for larger shows. Attend a few shows and look for a style and color that you like and that match both you and your horse. You can buy ready-made clothes or have them made by a seamstress for a more personal look.

CLOTHES AND ACCESSORIES CAN MAKE OR BREAK THE PICTURE

Sorrels, chestnuts, red roans, and red dun horses look good with

Long-sleeve shirts and starched and neat pants are acceptable at open shows.

A vest changes the look of your outfit and saves you from buying a second outfit.

A jacket is suitable for larger shows. Notice the tasteful earrings.

Youths can wear a long-sleeve shirt...

...and add a vest for a new look.

earth tones. Try tans, browns, and cinnamon or khaki colors. A bay, black, or gray horse is complimented by blues, especially royal blue, or shades of purple. Some people don't look good in certain colors, which is why you need to match the color not only to your horse, but also to yourself. Red is another color that works well with black and gray horses, but again, you must be comfortable wearing red. Forest green, teal, or shades of yellow will match many different-colored horses if you show more than one horse.

As is true of any written work, by the time you read this book, the current styles may have changed. Go to a large show just to see what the contestants are wearing. What was the first-place winner wearing? Then find a current style that will make you feel good about yourself. A compliment or two on your choice of clothes from a fellow competitor will make your day. That little extra edge gained by knowing that your favorite outfit is attractive may be just enough to add that winning smile to your face.

WOMEN

Small, tasteful earrings, either posts or clip-ons, are always suitable. Earrings that dangle will draw attention to your movements and become a distraction rather than an attraction. The same is true for large, gaudy rings. Not only are they unsafe when working around horses, but they draw attention to your hand movement.

At a larger show, gloves are appropriate. Your goal is to *minimize* the movements of your cues, so gloves that match the color of the sleeves of your blouse are a good choice because they minimize the movement of your hands. Be sure that the sleeves of your shirt reach to your glove, leaving no skin showing between your sleeves and the gloves. An attractive pin is never out of place, but remember that you want to compliment, not distract. Your goal is a neat and attractive all-over look.

Pants should fit attractively without being extremely tight, and should reach to the top of your heels—not drag the ground. A belt with a western buckle completes the picture (unless you wear a long jacket—then it is not necessary).

Your hat should be the best you can afford. Have it carefully cleaned and shaped to match the current style, and box it when you are not using it. Felt hats are acceptable in winter and straw hats in summer. Your hat should fit your head and not fall into your eyes, nor should it be so small that it perches on top of your head. A hat is a fashion statement. You may be able to cut corners elsewhere, but not on your hat.

The current style in boots is a rounded toe with crepe heel. That may change at some point, so always keep your eyes open for the latest style. A boot that matches the color of your pants will draw less attention to your leg movements, but a neutral-color boot will work with more outfits.

As the seasons change, so will your clothes. While a long-sleeve shirt is mandatory when showing western, a lightweight shirt will be more comfortable in summer and something with a little more weight to it will help in cooler weather. Your choice of jackets will also change from summer to winter.

Women's hair should be neatly contained in a hair bag, or in a bun.

A bun is an easy way to contain long hair. Wear it under your western hat...

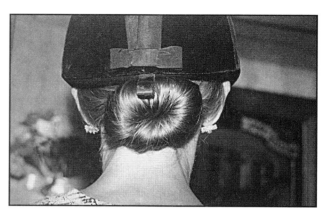

...or hunt cap...

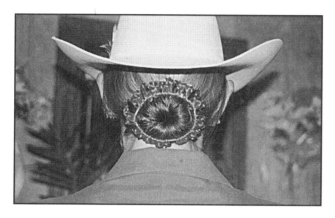

...or dress it up with a scrunchy.

Short hair is acceptable worn as is.

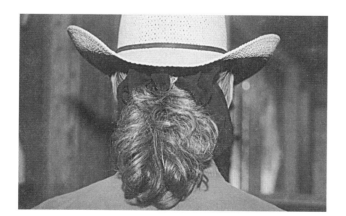

Medium length hair can be worn tied back. Be sure that your hair never covers your number. *It is very annoying to a judge to try to read a number covered by hair.*

Anything that flaps or blows, such as loose hair or a ponytail, is distracting. That would also include a large, baggy shirt or a tie that is too long and therefore moves distractingly. Neat and trim is the look of choice.

MEN

Men can wear starched jeans and a long-sleeve shirt. A tie is optional for a more formal look. Larger shows will require a well-fitting western jacket. Try a bright-colored, long-sleeved shirt to stand out from your more conservative competitors. Yellows, some shades of green or blue, teal, or even a rusty shade of orange can make you stand out. Wearing a patterned scarf will break up the solid color of a shirt. Choose a color that compliments both you and your horse.

A belt with a western buckle is mandatory, as are starched jeans. Once again, your hat should be the best you can afford, and it must be kept neat, clean, and shaped. Round-toed, crepe-soled boots are in, and be sure that your pants reach to the top of your heel. The old style, pointed-toe cowboy boots are currently out of style.

YOUTH

Youth styles are a little less formal than adults, although a touch of lipstick and perhaps a spot of rouge are acceptable for girls. Long-sleeve shirts, either plain or patterned, with a vest, and starched jeans and a western belt work for open shows. A jacket is appropriate at major shows.

For boys, a long-sleeve shirt in an attractive color that matches well with the horse, paired with

While your choice in English clothes may be limited to a jacket, breeches, hard hat, shirt with matching choker, boots and gloves, with small, tasteful earrings—all very conservative...

starched jeans and a belt with a western buckle, are adequate for the smaller shows. At a higher-level show, a jacket and tie would be more suitable. Hats that are shaped to match the current style, and clean, polished boots will finish the picture.

Clothes are meant to enhance an already professional performance. The best clothes will not win a class if you have not done your homework and taught both yourself and your horse the showmanship maneuvers. Yet, dressing in out-of-style or dated clothes says that you have not kept up with current trends, and styles do change. The showmanship class has become quite competitive, and to win you must keep current on styles, rules, and regulations. Be sure

...you can create a number of western outfits with one pair of good fitting pants just by changing the shirt, vest, or jacket and mixing and matching. Boots that are in style, plus the best hat that you can afford and a pair of gloves that match your outfit, complete the picture.

to see what's popular in the arena in your area today so that your clothes do not knock you down a placing or two. Whatever you choose, wherever you go, it should make *you* feel confident that your appearance is all it can be.

CHAPTER SIX

PRESENTATION

ALTHOUGH YOUR HORSE must be trained to perform the showmanship maneuvers and must be fit and meticulously clean with gleaming, shining tack, *showmanship is about you.* It is *your* attitude and *your* presentation of the horse that will win the class. Attitude comes from within. A fake, over-done smile or posture turns many judges off. It is not your attitude about yourself that wins the class—it is your attitude *about your horse.* It tells a judge that you have done your homework. You are proud of the horse that you are leading, and you want to win. Your attitude *must* convey that message. While you certainly must possess confidence to enter a ring, you must remember that you are showing the horse to the judge. You have to make him think that you believe your horse is worth a million dollars!

Your attention, however, must stay on the horse to be sure that he performs the pattern maneuvers correctly and holds his position—even in the lineup after you have performed your pattern. You must remember that there is a 1,000-pound animal on the end of your lead shank and he will not show himself. Some contestants are so concerned about their appearance that they forget to *show the horse.* Be sure that you do not make that mistake.

At the other extreme are the people who communicate through

This competitor is obviously ready to show. Her attitude and preparation are the first thing a judge will see and score accordingly. Photo by Cayla McKinney.

Showmanship is based on how well you show your horse. This competitor is so busy showing herself she is overlooking the small details of presentation that will cost her points. The judge will think that she doesn't care what her horse does as long as he looks at her.

Stand up tall and be proud of the horse that you show.

their body language that something is wrong, they are embarrassed to be leading the horse, or they're just too shy to be in this class. You can spot them without their ever uttering a word. Their horse won't behave, he does not perform as expected, he wouldn't load that morning, and so on. My point is that the person doesn't have to say

a word, yet you can know something is wrong.

Some people enter a showmanship class with a sour expression on their face. Maybe their horse refused to set up just prior to entering the ring, stepped on their toe, or began calling for a stablemate. Maybe their body language made the horse nervous. (A horse can sense nervousness and will become nervous himself.) Sometimes a contestant takes a look at the competition and knows, even before he enters the ring, that he and his horse are not good enough to win. Letting any of the above affect your attitude will almost certainly cost you a win before you ever start to perform.

You might look at your horse and think that you are ready to enter the arena, but if your attitude does not "shout" that you are ready and have the very best horse in the arena, you are setting yourself up for less than a blue ribbon. You have to enter the gate with the expectation of winning, and you must *hold that attitude throughout the entire class.* Then, even if you do not win the class, you will have given it your very best shot, and it will show in your attitude.

Remember, though, that if you don't win, or even place, do not let that affect your attitude. Good sportsmanship is a must! A judge will remember a poor sport for the rest of the day, and possibly even at future shows. Take whatever ribbon you get, smile, thank the ring steward, and go home to practice for the next show.

At any show, you are paying, through your entry fee, for a judge's opinion on a given day. Everyone hopes that the show committee hires a reputable judge who knows the classes and how to judge them, but that is not always the case. Be a good sport in any case. Smile, and go on to the next show.

When I have judged showmanship classes myself, I have placed contestants with a *minor* flaw in their pattern over others who performed a more correct pattern because the former had the attitude that said to me, "My horse is worth a million dollars. Don't you wish he were yours?"

Little things can affect which pair gets the blue ribbon. One horse might be more fit than another, or he might have a certain charisma that says he enjoys what he is doing. Or the handler may have asked correctly, but the horse took one extra step. If you or your horse make a mistake, keep showing to the best of your ability (and keep smiling). It may not affect your score as much as you think. Do your homework. Train your horse. Know that your horse will do what you ask of him, when you ask it of him. Be proud of his looks, his cleanliness, his manners, and his ring presence. Be proud of yourself—your clothes, your looks, your smile, and the time you've spent learning the showmanship maneuvers. All of those items are the key to a winning look.

SHOWMANSHIP IS PRESENTATION

Besides your attitude, your *presentation* of the horse will win or lose a class for you. Your attitude says that you are *capable* of winning this class; your *presentation* shows that you have trained the horse to perform the maneuvers correctly. You have studied the rules and are

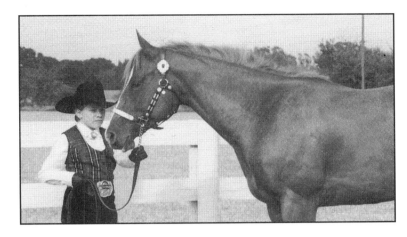

Look at the difference that...

...a good attitude and a smile make.

prepared to put your best foot forward.

SHOW YOUR HORSE TO HIS BEST ABILITY

You must present your horse to show his best. If you use a certain cue to make your horse perform, such as to trot alongside you, don't change the way that you ask on the day of the show.

Know your horse! If he tends to fidget when you hesitate, don't hesitate—make each maneuver flow from one to the next. Don't give him an opportunity to fidget or

A grooming box filled with supplies.

DO YOUR HOMEWORK

A good showmanship pair is like a couple that dances extremely well together. Most people, when dancing with a new partner, make a few mistakes—until they become so comfortable with each other that they know each other's every move. If, for some reason, one or the other of the partners makes a slight misstep or gets a half-step ahead or behind the other, the remaining partner can correct the mistake without anyone knowing that it was not performed exactly as they had planned. That is your goal with a showmanship horse.

Presentation of your horse includes, but is not limited to, cleanliness. You must clip his ears, his face, his chin, his bridle path, and his legs. Remove his chestnuts. Soak them with water, or remove them after a bath. It may take a few times before you get them down to skin level, so start well ahead of your first show.

Keep the tangles and burrs out of your horse's tail, and keep conditioner on it. Band his mane and black his hooves (rules permitting). You want your horse to look his absolute best—as if he is ready to enter a beauty pageant.

Be sure that his halter fits correctly and is adjusted properly. The leather must be clean and the silver, sparkling and shiny. An incorrect fit or adjustment tells a judge that you do not care enough to take the time to fit your halter to the horse. If you are not sure how to adjust it properly, ask for help.

A chain lead shank has become the accepted standard by which to show your horse. Be sure that he will perform with the chain under his chin. Some horses, when

perform in an unacceptable manner. Know what cues and signals you have taught him (or those he was taught previously), and show him to his best ability. If he has been taught to set up using a certain sequence of cues, be sure that you use that sequence. Use common sense. Never use the show ring to try a new method—save the trial-and-error sessions for at home when you are schooling your horse. Don't watch another competitor and decide at the last minute to see if your horse will obey the way that his horse does. Use your tried-and-true method at a show. Show your horse in the manner that he has become accustomed to at home. You cannot expect a horse to perform well if you do not put time in at home schooling him on these maneuvers. Showmanship has become so competitive that only those who train and polish their presentation will leave the arena with a blue ribbon.

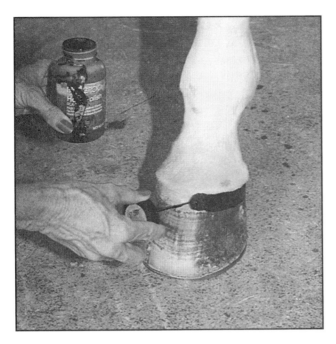

Draw a neat line of hoof black around the coronary band.

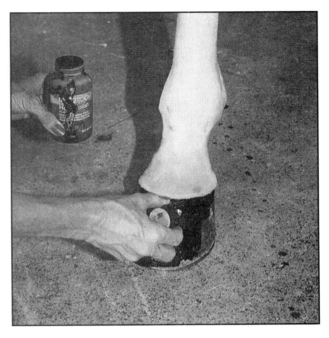

Work down to cover the hoof.

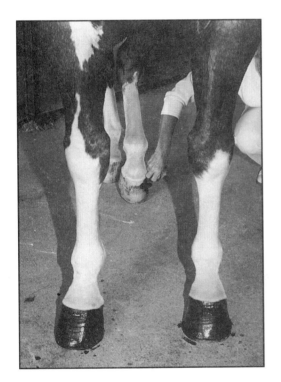

Correctly blackened hooves.

Use a halter that fits properly.

given a tug from the chain the first time, will set back and pull. A chain puts pressure in an area that a horse may not be used to until you teach him to accept pressure there. Use your show equipment at home a time or two before entering your first class. There is nothing worse than getting to a show and finding that your halter doesn't fit, your horse panics with a chain under his nose, or the snap on your lead line no longer snaps.

Your own clothes must be neat, and they should match the horse's color rather than clash. Choose a look, color, and style that is complimentary to both you and your horse. Wear a hat that is currently in style. Fads come and go. If you want to be competitive, you must keep up with the current styles. Keep your boots polished. Don't show in the boots that you use to muck stalls. Take a clean cloth and wipe any dust or mud from your boots just before you enter the ring. Wear a style of boot that is currently accepted. Keep everything neat and clean, and prepare yourself and your horse to the best of your ability. (I once won a large showmanship class with huge grass stains up and down both legs, but don't chance it! My horse spooked at a goat that was stalled alongside the lane that we used to enter the arena at a 4-H show. She knocked me flat on my face. I did not have time to change, nor did I bring extra pants with me. I caught my horse and went into the ring with a smile on my face and won the class. Attitude does count!)

BRING A SHOWMANSHIP BUCKET

Carry a showmanship bucket to the entrance of the arena so that you can do some last-minute pol-

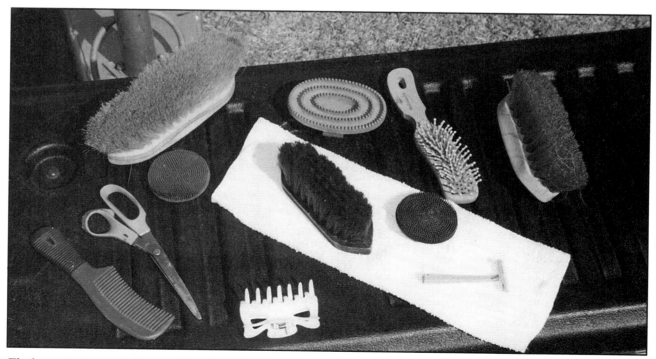

The bare minimum of what you'll need on show day. Left to right, back row: body brush, rubber curry, mane and tail brush; front row: mane comb, scissors, mane clip, soft brush, rubber face curry, razor and clean towel.

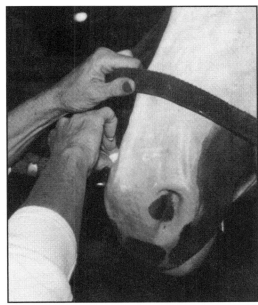

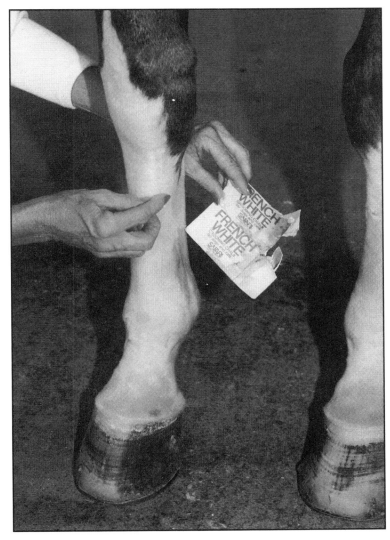

Wipe the face and corners of the eyes with a clean, soft cloth.

Use French White® chalk (or baby powder or corn starch) to whiten the face or legs.

ishing before you enter the arena. Leave nothing to chance! Your bucket or kit should contain a clean, soft brush, a mane and tail brush, a body brush, a curry, soft white towels or cloths, fly spray, face makeup, hoof black, Show Sheen® or some type of coat polish, and French White® grooming chalk. And don't use these showmanship supplies at home. Brushes won't stay clean. Supplies are depleted and not replenished, or hoof black is accidentally left open and dries up.

Make any needed last-minute repairs to your horse before you enter the arena. Wipe his nose, wipe under his tail, and dust off his body with the clean towel. Look him over closely to see if anything needs a last-minute touch-up. Remember, you are out to win this class, so put your best effort into it.

Presentation of your horse is everything in this class. (Notice there is a leg under each quarter of the horse.) Misty Seven, owned by the author. Photo by Cayla McKinney.

CHAPTER SEVEN

THE QUARTER METHOD

THE QUARTER METHOD of showing at halter has become the accepted standard today. The art of showing in showmanship or at halter is much like a dance. When your partner, in this case the judge, moves, you must move to the appropriate position. However, unlike a dance, the quarter method of showing is based on safety—safety for you, because you have control of the horse's head through the correct use of your lead line, and safety for the judge. If you miss a step in a dance, you might look silly or get an annoyed look from your partner. If you miss a step when showing a 1,000-pound horse and he becomes fractious, being in the wrong position can result in serious harm to the judge.

If you show (or plan to show) in showmanship or halter classes, learn to use the quarter method. It is so named because the horse is sectioned in four equal quarter parts.

WHERE ARE THE QUARTERS?

First, a line is drawn straight down the middle of the horse from his nose to his tail. Then a second line is drawn from his left side to his right side, directly behind his withers, sectioning the horse into four quarters. The sections of the horse are numbered as follows:

I—right front (off).

II—right hind (off).

III—left hind (near).

IV—left front (near).

THE MECHANICS OF THE METHOD

Picture a merry-go-round horse with a pole centered right behind his withers and you will understand the mechanics behind the use of the quarter method. If you pulled the head of the horse on the merry-go-round toward you, where would his hind end go? It would swing away from you, or in the opposite direction. The same is true of your living, breathing horse. When you pull his head toward you, his hindquarters and rump swing in the opposite direction, away from the judge when he is standing on the same side of the horse as you. Therefore, the safest place for a judge (or a vet, farrier, or innocent bystander) to be when he is

The Correct Positions for Each Quarter

1) *To understand the quarter method of showing, we've divided this horse into four quarters. When the judge is in the right front quarter, the exhibitor is in the left front quarter, giving the judge an unobstructed view of the horse.*

2) *As the judge moves into the right rear quarter, the exhibitor moves to the right front quarter.*

3) *As the judge passes into the left rear quarter, the exhibitor crosses the front of the horse in three steps and moves back into the left front quarter of the horse.*

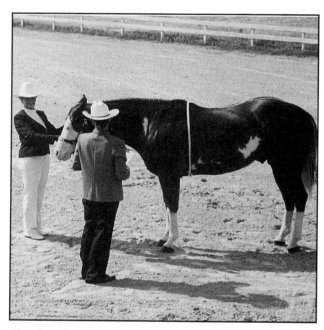

4) *When the judge crosses the center line and moves into the left front quarter of the horse, the exhibitor crosses into the right front quarter of the horse and remains there until the judge either directs the exhibitor to perform a maneuver (as called for on the pattern) or crosses the center line of the front of the horse and moves into the right front quarter, in which case the exhibitor must cross back to the left front quarter. Remember that the quarter method holds true as the judge moves down the line of exhibitors. You must always give him an unobstructed view, even as he judges the next horse. He may look back to see if you are still showing your horse. Be sure that he has an unobstructed view of the horse at all times.*

standing near the hindquarters of a horse is on the same side as the handler. If the judge stood on the opposite (right) side of the horse near the hindquarters while the handler is in the correct leading position, the horse's hindquarters would swing to the right (directly *into* the judge) if the horse's head was pulled toward the handler.

When the judge is in front of the withers of the horse, the handler stands on the opposite side from the judge. When the horse's head is pulled toward the handler, it moves away from the judge, thus avoiding a potentially dangerous situation. If the judge stands on the left side of the horse in front of the withers, the handler must move to the right side of the horse. Not only does this keep the judge safe, it allows him an unobstructed view of the front of the horse. Since *you* are being judged on your ability to show a horse correctly and to the best advantage, you must never block the horse from the judge's view.

When the judge moves to the right side of the horse near his hindquarters, you must then move to the right side of the horse. If your horse becomes fractious and you pull his head toward you, his rump will swing harmlessly to the left (or in the opposite direction), away from the judge. If the judge moves to the left side of the horse near his hindquarters, you must then also move to the left side of the horse. If the judge moves to the right front of the horse, you move to the left front of the horse so that you can move the horse's head away from the judge. If the judge moves to the left front of the horse, you move to the right side of the horse so that, once again, you can pull the horse's head

toward you and away from the judge.

When the judge is in position I (right front), where many judges start their evaluation of a horse, you should be in IV (left front). As the judge moves to II (right hind), you should take three steps—one step over with your left foot, another step across your left foot with your right foot, then a final step in which you bring your left foot together with your right foot. This is the correct way to move across the front of the horse to position I (right front).

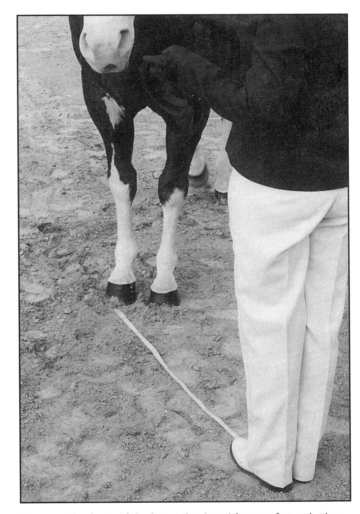

To cross the front of the horse, begin with your feet pointing at the horse's right front hoof as shown. Also, when presenting your horse to the judge, you should always point your feet toward the opposite front hoof.

1) Ready to begin the crossover steps. The steps in these photos are exaggerated. for

2) Step out with your left foot to the center of your horse's nose.

3) Cross your right foot in front of your left foot.

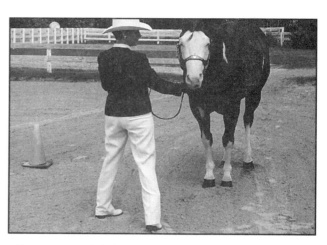

4) Move your left foot behind; plant and pivot it. Finally, bring your right foot into place beside your left foot and stand square.

5) You are now in line with the horse's left front foot, with your feet pointing at it. Reverse these steps when you need to cross back to the other side of the horse.

6) As you make the crossover step as described in photo 2, above, the lead shank passes under the horse's nose.

When the judge moves to III (left hind), you take those same steps, starting this time with your right foot, to get back to position IV (left front). And, when the judge moves to IV (left front), you move back to position I (right front), again using those same steps.

These steps around the horse should look like a dance; your position and smoothness will make or break the picture that the judge sees. Not only must you make the correct steps, but you must have an attitude that shows in your manner as well. A natural smile lets the judge know that you have done your homework and are proud of the horse you are leading. A fake, overdone smile only detracts from the polished, professional picture that you must present if you wish to do well in this class.

WATCH THE JUDGE, WATCH THE HORSE

While showing, you must stay alert and be aware of the position of the judge at all times. Remember, too, that you are showing the horse, not yourself. Correct any mistakes he makes as quickly, yet as unobtrusively, as possible. Teach your horse to back up as readily as he walks forward and to perform the 360-degree or 180-degree turn in place. (See the following chapter, "Teaching the Basic Maneuvers.")

Learn to stand up straight and look at the judge. As you step away from the horse so that the judge may view him, your toes (and therefore your entire body) should always be pointed toward the horse's right front foot. (When you are in position IV, left front.)

Smile, be alert, pay attention, and show your horse to the best of your ability. Looking at the ground or having a subdued, defeated look on your face says to the judge that you are embarrassed or afraid. In order to place well in a showmanship class, you need to exude pride and a positive attitude

Remember: your horse is not being judged—he is merely a prop that allows you to demonstrate the extent of your ability to show a horse to his best potential. *You* are being judged on the manner in which you show the horse.

PRACTICE DAILY

A well-trained horse that sets up easily in a square position and leads alongside you at both the walk and trot is obviously an asset in this class. Training a horse to lead and to set up correctly is something that almost anyone can do successfully if you put in your time and practice daily. Teaching a horse to perform the 360-degree turn may take a bit more practice, but again, almost every horse can be taught to perform well if you take the time to train him.

THE RESULT: GOOD GROUND MANNERS

For basic safety reasons, every horse should learn good ground manners, whether or not you plan to show him. For that reason alone, you should study the mechanics of the quarter method. Your farrier and vet will thank you for it. And who knows, being in the right place at the right time might just prevent an accident.

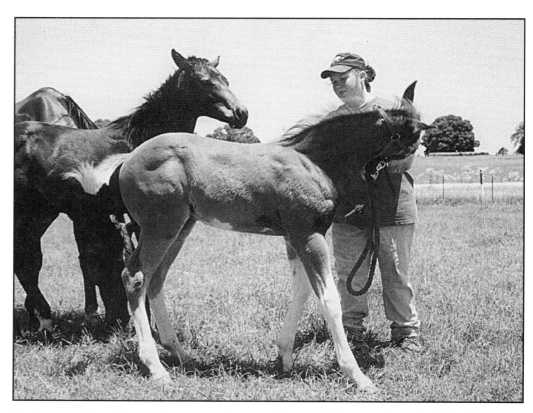

Teach your colt good ground manners at your earliest possible convenience. It will make any horse more enjoyable to work around. Kimberly Baldwin is holding SC Dee's Lucky Dancer, owned by the author.

CHAPTER EIGHT

TEACHING THE MANEUVERS

When practicing at home, don't use your show halter, but do use a chain to prepare your horse to obey the signals given by a chain under his chin. Don't wait until show day to introduce your horse to the chain! And don't wait until show day to be sure that your show halter fits correctly and has all the necessary holes punched to adjust it to fit your horse. Be prepared!

SHOWMANSHIP IS JUDGED on a handler's ability to show his horse. The horse is merely a prop that you use to show your expertise and ability. Before you enter your first showmanship class, your horse must learn to stand, often for long periods of time, without fidgeting or moving. Not only must he stand, he must stand with his hooves squarely underneath him and learn to hold that position quietly. He must lead well, both at the walk and the jog, and move confidently beside you—without trying to drag you with him or having you pull him along. He must back up on command as easily as he moves forward. And he must learn the proper way to execute a turn in place and to pivot on his right hind leg without walking out of the turn.

WHOA!

One of the first things to teach a horse that is headed for a showmanship class is the meaning of the word "whoa!" When you begin teaching this lesson, make it easy for your horse to differentiate between being led from barn to turnout area and working on specific showmanship maneuvers. Put a chain under his nose while you are training for showmanship. Use a chain that is long enough to run under the chin and up the side of the cheek-piece on the opposite side. Fasten the snap in the upper ring of the halter. Using a chain in this manner will keep your halter in place without twisting on the horse's face. If you have a horse that is pushy while being led (often caused by lack of respect for his handler), you can give a quick, sharp tug and release when you say the word "whoa!" until the horse understands that when you say "whoa!" you mean "whoa!" The horse should stop and stand. (Anytime you use a chain shank under a horse's nose, be sure to give a tug and release—an immediate release is extremely important.) Your horse must know and respect the word "whoa!"

When the horse stops, his throat latch should be in line with your shoulder. He should not walk past you, try to turn either left or right, nor throw his hip out in either direction. Teach your horse that you will correct him if he chooses to disobey you or tries to fool around. An additional benefit of making your horse obey your cues from the ground is that respect gained on the ground will carry over to work under saddle.

SETTING UP

Once a horse obeys the whoa command, teach him to set up square. In the initial training, first say "whoa!" to ask the horse to halt. Use the lead line to move the horse forward or backward until the left (or near) back leg is lined up with his right leg. The right hind leg remains stationary and you set the

horse around that leg. Say, for example, that the left hind leg is a bit too far forward. You want to move only the left hind foot so that it lines up with the right hind foot. With your hand close to the halter, but not on the chain, push your lead slightly toward the left hind, the foot you want to move. He should begin to move that foot backward. Because you didn't lift the lead line to move the back leg, you encourage the horse's front end to stay solidly on the ground. When the left foot moves backward, in line with the right foot, say "stand" and give a slight downward pull on your lead shank to plant the left hind foot. Now praise the horse so he knows that he did what you asked.

Hand place the horse's front legs in a square position for the first few days and praise him for standing in this square position. Say "stand," rub the horse's neck, and let him rest. Let him think that standing with his feet in a square position is a nice place to be and that he will be rewarded for it.

After a few days of this you can begin to use the lead shank to ask the horse to adjust his front feet. The method is basically the same as with the hind feet, except that you *lift* the horse's head a bit more to encourage a front foot to come up and move forward. Lifting the horse's head lightens his front end, sending his weight rearward. This frees his front end so that he can move his front leg into place.

To move the left front foot, keep your lead line parallel to the left side of his body and ask him to move that foot forward or backward. To move a right front leg, your lead line will angle toward the right rear of the horse and will

1) *Lead your horse and ask him to stop. You can look at your horse to see if he is correct at home, but do not look at him when showing!*

4) *Touching a horse's hooves with your feet might be accept- able in the initial stages of training, but it is not acceptable in showmanship classes. (You are allowed to set up this way in halter classes.) Teach your horse to set up from your lead shank cues.*

2) *To set him up in the square position, remember that his right rear foot remains stationary and you set the other feet to match his right rear. When the horse moves his foot to the correct position, give a slight downward tug on the lead shank to "set" the foot.*

5) *Move the right front hoof to the correct position. Be sure your horse is neither camped out (legs too far apart front to back) nor too close underneath the horse, making it appear as if he is perched on a stool. Enlist the help of a friend if necessary and step back to look to see if each leg is under each quarter of the horse.*

3) *Move the left rear so it squares up with the right rear hoof.*

6) *The end result is a horse that stands squarely, with a leg under each quarter.*

again move the horse forward or backward so that the right front lines up with the left front.

If your horse moves out of square before you have asked him to move, give a quick tug and release on the chain (a correction) and immediately put him back in position as you repeat the stand command. If a horse moves, *immediately* correct him and *immediately* put him back in the correct position. Otherwise, he will not understand the correction or know how to avoid it in the future. He must learn the proper response to your stand command.

In the initial lessons, ask the horse to hold this square position for only one to two minutes while you praise him with a verbal "good boy." Then, lead him forward and ask him to set up again. Most horses learn quickly that the verbal praise means that they have done well and that they should try to repeat such behavior in the future.

Your goal is to have the horse halt squarely on your whoa command (or on your nonverbal command in the finished stages). When you stop, stay by the horse's head in a leading position until he stops. You can see him in your peripheral vision. Then, take a step forward with your left foot, pivot to face the horse, and bring your right foot square with your left foot. Both of your feet should now be aimed at the horse's right front hoof.

When a horse stops correctly, both hind feet should be square. You might have to adjust a front hoof. With enough practice, eventually the horse will adjust his feet without you having to do a thing. It will become a habit for him to stop and square up.

Practice walking in the same cadence as your horse. You should walk in four-four time. In other words, walk: one, two, three, four; one, two, three, four.

LEADING CORRECTLY

The most basic of the showmanship maneuvers is to lead your horse correctly beside you. His throat latch should be in line with your shoulder. He should not lag behind you, nor should he surge in front of you. He should move briskly alongside you and travel in a straight line. He should not swing his hip to the outside nor cock his head to you. Beware of holding your lead line too short or holding too closely to the horse's halter, because you can inadvertently pull the horse's head toward you and force him to travel with his head cocked to you. Because the showmanship class began as a way to teach handlers to show in a halter class, a judge wants to see how the horse travels and if he tracks in a straight line. A horse cannot track in a straight line

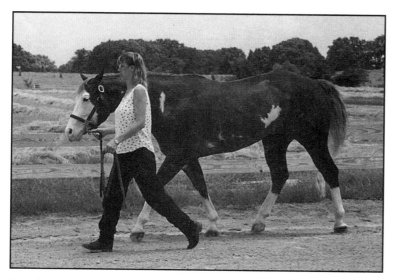

Don't drag your horse. Teach him to lead beside you. You should be in line with his throat latch as you lead him.

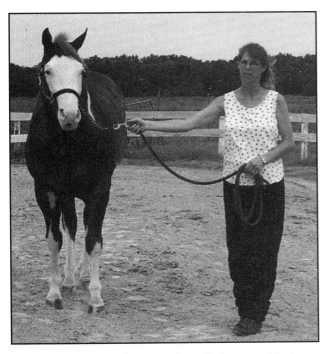

This exhibitor is too far away from the horse and lacks control.

Here, her hand is too close to the horse, yet her body is too far from the horse. Find a happy medium between these two extremes.

if you pull his head toward you. Your horse should lead beside you with a reasonably loose line, but not one so long that it is sloppy. Your hand should be three to four inches from his halter. He must have enough room to travel correctly. You should not be dragged along by your horse. That is a sign of a lack of training or a lack of respect, and points will be deducted. Your horse must learn to move briskly and energetically beside you—not amble or drag his toes along the ground. Your horse should be alert and obedient to your every cue. A horse that lags alongside his handler reminds you of the hack horses on a stable line. They do not have to pay attention to the rider—they just follow the horse in front of them. On the other hand, a horse that travels briskly beside you reminds you of a finely tuned reining horse, alert to your every command.

If your horse does not lead alertly alongside you or tries to lag behind you, carry a buggy whip for a day or two. It may help him to understand that lagging is unacceptable. This will help him learn to move forward more readily than pulling on the chain under his chin. If you do choose to use the chain under his chin, again, be sure that you give little tugs and releases. A steady pull on a chain under a horse's nose can cause him to rear and perhaps go over backward.

Instead of using a chain, you can also run a rope lead line under the horse's chin, threading it through the rings of the halter in the same method that you would use with a chain. This is a good way to prepare both you and the horse for using a chain. It is especially beneficial if you've never used a chain before, or for teaching a youth exhibitor.

To teach the horse to walk off on your body cues, lean slightly forward with your shoulders to cue him to begin to walk. *Don't move until the horse moves.* As he gains in understanding of this maneuver, refine your cue so that you do not lean forward so much that it is obvious. In time, your horse will learn to move forward as you bring your hand forward, before you move your shoulders. Train consistently.

Once a horse leads well, ask him to lead beside you, set up squarely, and walk forward again. Each time the horse moves forward from the square position before you ask him, give a corrective tug on the chain and *immediately* put him back in a square position. If your horse moves without being told and you do not immediately put him back in that position, how is he to know what he is being corrected for? Remember—you have three seconds to correct a horse. Waiting longer leaves him confused as to what he did wrong. Failing to immediately put him back in the correct position

will also confuse him. In order for a horse to learn, you must talk to him in a language that he can understand. A corrective snap on the chain when he moves out of the stand position, followed by being put back in the correct stand position, is easy for him to understand. He thinks, "I moved my feet and got corrected. When my feet were in that square position, my owner was happy and rubbed my neck and I got to rest."

When your horse will stand squarely on command, switch your position to the right, or off side, of the horse. You must be sure that he will hold his position while you stand on the off side and while you move from left to right. Don't assume that because the horse will stand when you are on his left side, he will stand when you are on the right side. Practice *at home* standing on both sides.

JOGGING

To teach your horse to jog alongside you, it is helpful to first

Teach your horse to jog briskly along beside you. You should take "trotting" steps when your horse trots.

teach him to obey a verbal cluck as his cue to jog in the round pen (or on a longe line). Once he understands this signal to jog, he probably will jog when you cluck while leading him. If he doesn't, use a buggy whip to urge him forward. Hold it in your left hand and reach around behind with the whip to encourage the horse to move out. As with walking, your horse must learn to jog without any visible cues from you—that is your ultimate goal.

I teach my horses to jog in the barn aisle because they are confined on either side and can't swing their hip away from me and avoid the tap of the whip. If you don't have this available to you, jog with the horse alongside a fence, so that the fence controls one side of the horse. Because you are on the left side of the horse, you will block his movement to the left and the fence will block him from moving to the right.

Cluck to ask your horse to jog. If he doesn't jog, reach as far back with your whip as you can and tap his hindquarters. Be careful at this point. Some horses will leap forward the first time or two that they feel the whip. Be sure *not to* shank the horse back even if he leaps forward, or he will think you are telling him not to jog or go faster. He will interpret the jerk on the shank as a correction. Instead, allow him to move forward at whatever pace he chooses the first few times. Reward the forward movement.

With an extremely flighty horse, you may need to first teach him that the whip is an aid and not to be feared. Spend as much time as it takes for him to accept a whip being rubbed over his body

After your horse has jogged forward for twenty to forty feet,

Your horse should plant his right hind pivot foot to do a 90-, 180-, or a 360-degree turn in place.

Use your hand or a sweat scraper to increase the horse's impulsion to move around the turn with energy. Keep the horse's body aligned from head to tail.

He should cross over with his left front foot in front of his right front as he pivots or turns in place.

ease him back down to a walk and praise him. Let him know that he did the right thing by jogging alongside you. Then repeat the steps and ask again. Ask him to jog three or four times on the first day, then put him up or go on to something else. Don't drill, drill, drill, or your horse will think that he has done something wrong. Training takes time.

After a few days, you may no longer need to tap your horse with the whip, but you may want to carry it for a few days as you ask him to jog. As he begins to jog alongside you in response to your cluck and jogging steps, try to omit the whip. If he will not jog, immediately get your whip and reinforce that he must jog when you ask him. Ask without the whip again the following day, and continue using this method until the horse will jog readily on command and no longer needs the verbal cluck. The ideal showmanship horse works totally off of non-verbal body language!

TEACHING THE PIVOT

Now that your horse will lead readily alongside you and will increase his speed to a jog, he is ready to learn to turn in place, or to perform the 360. To do this correctly, your horse must move with impulsion, or energy. He must learn to hold his hind pivot foot in one spot, much like when performing a spin in a reining class, and to cross over with his left front leg. If a cluck alone doesn't increase his energy, use the rounded backside of a metal sweat scraper to tap his shoulder. It is just the right length and fits comfortably in your hand. Your horse must walk forward with energy around this turn. Your hand on the lead line should be a few inches from the halter so that you have control of his head. Ask him to move slightly forward and around. Do not let the horse bend his neck around the turn. The goal is for the horse to remain straight throughout his body and cross over with the left front leg as he uses his right hind leg to pivot. You should face the horse between his head and his shoulder so that you can encourage him to move away from you.

Use a fence to teach your horse to back straight. Remember that you must turn and face your horse when you ask him to back up. You control the direction of the horse's rearward movement by directing his hindquarters. His hindquarters lead the direction of the back up. Practice moving backward between cones after you learn to keep him moving backward along the fence in a straight line.

As you ask the horse to halt from the walk, lift your lead line to set him back on his hocks (transferring his weight to the rear), then go directly into the turn. Use the lead line to guide the horse's head slightly

Showmanship is not for just for women. Many men also compete. And, even if you never enter a showmanship class, teaching your horse the showmanship maneuvers makes him more mannerly and respectful.

forward and to the right and the sweat scraper to tap his shoulder so that he moves away from pressure and crosses over to the right. If he tries to bring his left front leg *behind* his right front leg to make the turn, you will know that you need more *forward* energy. Use your sweat scraper to tap him to increase his energy level. It will take practice for a horse to make a complete turn in place, so start by asking him to cross over for one or two steps, then three and four steps, then a 180 degree turn. Finally, increase the steps until he does a complete 360. Be sure to praise him for each correct step so that he understands what you are asking. At the end of a month or two he should be making a complete turn in place.

Your position can make or break the 360. Never ask the horse to back into the pivot—that will cause him to step behind, not in

front of, the right front foot with his left front foot. You must travel in a perfectly round circle, allowing the horse enough room to perform the 360. If you walk in an oval or oblong shape, your horse will travel in an oval or oblong shape and lose form!

LEARNING TO BACK UP

In addition to the above maneuvers, your horse must back up readily from the ground. Your sweat scraper can once again be used to tap his chest if he doesn't back up readily from your lead-line cue alone. To begin, teach your horse to back straight by asking him to back up along a fence or down the barn aisle. Put the horse next to the fence so that, once again, the fence helps to keep the horse in position. With the chain under his chin, give little tugs and releases to ask him to move backward. If he

If a pattern asks you to walk at a cone, begin walking when your horse's front feet are even with the cone. Photo by Cayla McKinney.

doesn't respond to that, use your sweat scraper to tap his chest until he takes the first step backward. Praise him for that one step to tell him that he did the right thing. Then ask for one step again. Once he masters backing up one step at a time, you can ask for two, then three, and so on. Don't be in a hurry. Break each training segment down into small pieces and build on each previously learned step. The horse must learn to back from slight lead-line pressure only.

One of the newer maneuvers in showmanship is backing around or through markers or cones. You might be asked to back in a circle around a cone or to back in and around three cones. Teach your horse to move his hip first—that is what leads in the backup. To ask your horse to move backward to the right, tip his head to the left, and vice versa. Practice until you can put your horse in any position, forward and backward, that you want.

With consistent practice, as well as proper conditioning, your horse should be ready to master the showmanship class. He will have better ground manners, and the two of you will enjoy a better relationship as you work toward bringing home that once-elusive trophy.

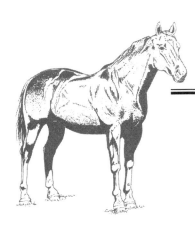

CHAPTER NINE

THE PATTERNS

THE SHOWMANSHIP CLASS was originally based on teaching the amateur how to show a halter horse. While that is still true today, patterns have become increasingly more complicated and intricate. For example, a common pattern of the 1970s was to walk to the judge, set up, turn, and trot back to the line-up. The showmanship patterns that are popular today often require that you walk, trot, perform a 180, 270, or 360 degree turn, back your horse and set him up with a minimum of cues in three seconds or less. All this while you are expected to maintain your poise and present a pleasing, attractive and efficient picture.

Once your horse will lead correctly beside you and you have taught him to set up, to perform the 360-degree turn in place, and to back up readily, you are ready to try a pattern. Don't try to learn just one pattern because patterns vary from show to show and from judge to judge.

There are so many combinations and variations of patterns that to discuss every possible one would take up this entire book—and I would still miss a few. Yet, once your horse learns the basic show-manship *maneuvers*, your goal is to be able to put them together in whatever pattern might be called for at a show. Your training program should enable your horse to breeze right through the maneuvers—in whatever order they might be listed. Teaching a horse to perform a set *pattern*, rather than to obey a *command*, is not really *training* a horse. It is teaching him to perform by rote. Instead, teach your horse to obey your cues for each individual exercise; then he will be ready for any pattern the judge requests at a show.

READ THE PATTERN

The first order of business at a show, after entering and settling in, is to read the pattern for your class. Understand exactly what it says. Ask if you're unsure. Try to analyze what the judge wants. For example, "Back up five steps," indicates that the judge is probably a stickler for *perfection and precision*. If he says "back up five steps," he means five steps—not six or three or seven. Therefore, remember that you must count your horse's steps as he moves in reverse—one, two, three, four, five. If the pattern calls for a

270 degree turn, it means 270 degrees—not 360 degrees, and not 210 degrees—but 270 degrees (three-quarters of a circle). Your horse must stop precisely when he hits the three-quarter mark

If a pattern calls for you to stop at a cone, it means for you to stop *at (even with)* the cone. Suppose, however, your next maneuver is a 360-degree turn. You must plan your stop far enough away from the cone that it will not interfere with your horse's performance. For example, if you are on the left side of a cone and the pattern calls for a 360-degree turn to the right, you must stop a horse-length away from the cone so that your horse can turn correctly (with his body in a straight line) and not end up on top of the cone or knock it over.

Always take time at a show to think ahead and plan your pattern. If a pattern calls for you to walk or jog to a cone and then back to a pre-determined spot before making a 90-degree turn toward the judge, be sure that you stop backing with your horse's rear end in line with the judge. Then, when you make the ninety-degree turn, your horse's body will be lined up straight, facing the judge. When you walk toward him, your horse will not have to veer or swerve to line up correctly. You should always place yourself so that your *horse* is walking *directly at the judge*. Your right shoulder should line up with the judge's right shoulder.

PERFORM PATTERNS WITH PRECISION

Patterns must be executed exactly as written. Many of today's patterns use cones as markers, and getting too close or too far from the cone will disrupt that maneuver. An example: You do a 360-degree turn and bump into the cone—a big penalty. If you lose the flow in one maneuver, it often disrupts your next maneuver, if not the balance of your entire pattern. The whole pattern must flow from one segment to the next.

If the judge asks you to walk to a cone, back up three steps, then trot to the next cone, he does not want to see your horse hesitate or fidget between the back up and the trot, or between the walk and the back up. Your horse must move willingly from one movement to the next with no sign of resentment or confusion. Your horse cannot crowd you or shy away from you. He must respect, not fear, you and he must move willingly with you so that the two of you look like a team—much like a couple that has danced together for years.

You *must* put your time in at home, teaching your horse to lead, to set up, and to basically do *what you ask, when you ask*.

Most patterns require that you walk either toward or away from the judge. Always make certain that your *horse*—not you—is directly in line with the judge! Be sure that you travel in a straight line. Pick a point at eye level or above at the opposite end of the arena and walk directly toward it. You might choose a visual aid such as a trailer window, a high limb on a small tree, a certain fence post, or any number of other objects that are directly in front of you but some distance away. You cannot look at the ground or to the left or right. If you look at the ground, you can't see where you are going, and it will look to a judge as if you are unsure of yourself. If you look to the left, your body will naturally veer to the left. The same is true of looking to the right. Look up, straight ahead, and smile. Hold the lead line correctly so that you do not tip your horse's head to either side.

As you look ahead, you can also see where the marker or cone for your next maneuver is situated. If you are required to stop at the cone and set your horse up for the judge, be sure that you know which side of the cone to be on. Many judges use this as a large criterion in their scoring. If your horse is required to do a 360-degree turn *at or near a cone,* study the pattern carefully to see if the judge wants your horse to start the 360 before or at the side of the cone. If you stop with your horse's hind end *at the cone,* you will run into or knock the cone down as you finish the turn. If you stop with your horse's head *directly beside the cone,* you will again hit the cone as you complete the 360-degree turn. Give your horse enough space to perform the 360 without knocking the cone down or shying away from it. You must read and understand the pattern before you enter the ring, and you must plan your pattern ahead of time!

THE VARIOUS MANEUVERS

The maneuvers that may be required are, but are not limited to, a 90-degree, 180-degree, 270-degree, or 360-degree turn in place. The ideal in this maneuver is for your horse to plant his inside, right hind leg and rotate around that, similar to when a reining horse spins to the right. His left front leg must cross over in front of (not behind) his right front leg. His planted (right) hind pivot foot should remain planted, or nearly so, as his entire body, which should stay straight from head to tail, pivots or rotates around that leg. A horse may have to lift and reposition that planted pivot leg or hoof, but the hoof's position should not change radically as if he were to step out of the turn.

A horse that leads correctly alongside you, with your shoulder at his throat latch at both the walk and jog, and that performs a 360 (or other turn) fluidly, will give you an edge over a competitor whose horse does not move as precisely. Your horse should back up as readily as he walks forward. He should set up and stand square in three seconds or less, with a minimum of adjustment from you. You must practice so that it becomes automatic for him to place his feet in a square position. (If you are showing a horse that is not a Paint or a Quarter Horse, check your breed-association rules on how or in what manner your horse should be set. For example, Arabs are set with their legs stretched and their head and neck extended. Read your rules.)

Your goal is to have your horse in the correct position in a matter of seconds. Teach your horse to hold that position whether you are on the left or right side of him. (See Chapter 7 on the quarter method of showing.) He must learn to hold this position for long periods of time. Although he doesn't have to remain alert with his ears perked for an entire class, standing out of position or with a hind leg cocked or resting will most certainly lower your score. As you move up to bigger and better classes, the number of entries will increase, and therefore the length of the class will increase. Prepare your horse at home. Ask him to stand correctly for five minutes and gradually increase the length of time to fifteen or twenty minutes at a stretch. (Remember, a really young horse will have a harder time mastering this than an older horse because of his shorter attention span.) When you have achieved this amount of control, you're ready to enter your first show.

PATTERNS

Now let's look at sample patterns and some common mistakes and how to avoid or correct them.

Pattern #1. Walk to the first cone. Perform a 360-degree turn. Trot to the judge and set up. When the judge releases you (by a nod of his head), do a 180-degree turn, trot back through the lineup, do another 180 turn, and set up in your original position.

Pattern #2. Trot to the first cone. Do a 360-degree turn. Walk to the second cone and do a ninety-degree turn. Walk to the judge and set up for inspection. When he releases you, back up five steps, do a ninety-degree turn, and trot back through the lineup, do a 180, and return to the line up.

Pattern #3. Walk to the first cone, trot to the judge, do a 360-degree turn, and set up. Then perform a 180-degree turn, trot to the fence (through the other horses), do another 180 and set up in your original position.

Pattern #4. Trot to the first cone and then walk to the second. Back up to the first (original) cone and do

a ninety-degree turn. Walk to the judge, and set up when dismissed Then walk past the judge to return to the lineup.

Most patterns will be a variant on one of these themes. They all combine certain elements: i.e, a 90-, 180- or 360-degree turn, a walk and jog, back up, and setup for inspection. Your horse must be comfortable with each of these maneuvers so that every element flows from one to the next. Your presentation must look polished and professional if you expect to win.

What exactly is the judge looking for in each of these patterns? Let's take them one by one and see how to make them flow.

SAMPLE PATTERN ONE

When the competitor in front of you gets part way through his pattern, walk your horse to the cone that marks the starting point of the pattern and set him up. As you wait for your turn to begin, your horse should stand squarely. His head should be at the cone, allowing you enough room to stand beside him if the cone is on the left. You should be facing the horse, with your toes facing his right front hoof, just as when you set up for inspection.

Turn only your head when you look at the judge. Don't twist from the waist up, and don't put an unnatural sway or arch in your back—it is unattractive and fake. Be sure to glance at your horse from time to time to be sure that he has not moved out of square or decided to rest or cock a hind leg. Keep your body straight—aligned from your shoulders to your heels. This will allow you to swivel only your head to glance at your horse or at the judge.

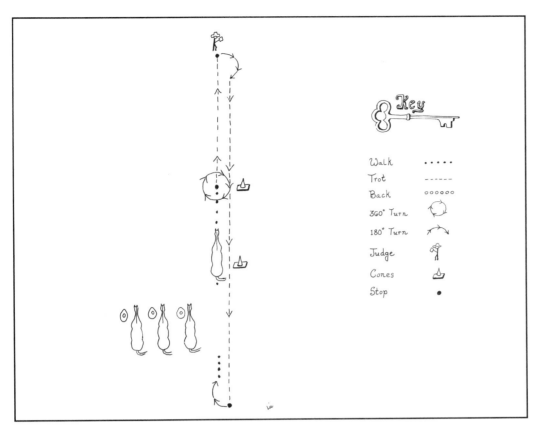

Pattern 1.

Key

Walk	· · · · ·
Trot	– – – – –
Back	ooooo
360° Turn	
180° Turn	
Judge	
Cones	
Stop	·

Keep the hand closest to the horse's halter on the leather of the lead line—never on the chain. Holding the chain itself is a major offense for safety reasons. If the horse pulled back or tried to pull away from you, the chain would be pulled through your hand and could leave you with a serious injury. Along the same line, don't hang onto your horse's head or nag at him with the lead line. You must allow him room to move with you naturally. If you force his head toward you as you walk, his hind end will swing out to the right. Your goal is to have your horse travel in a straight line, directly toward the judge. Applying constant pressure to the chain under a horse's chin causes pain, and most horses will react negatively.

Remember—anytime you use a chain under a horse's chin, you must leave the line loose and apply little tugs and releases if you need a correction. If you hang on the chain and pull, in all likelihood your horse will react by pulling backward. Then he could rear and might

Holding the chain instead of the leather of the lead line is penalized heavily in show-manship class. SC Splashsrobinboy.

even flip over. A chain under a horse's nose must be used correctly. By the time you are ready for your first showmanship class, your horse should be so in tune with your moves that he follows your body cues, and the lead line should stay slack throughout the entire class.

If your grip on the leather of the lead line is more than four inches from the horse's halter, the chain is too long. Either shorten the chain or buy a different lead line. As a quick fix, double the chain back through the ring at the top cheek piece of the halter and snap it to itself, as shown in the accompanying photo. It is neater and more desireable, however, to have the chain shortened.

If your horse makes a mistake, and your hand is too far from the horse, you will have to radically change your position to correct the horse. This literally screams to the judge that your horse has performed something incorrectly. If you keep your hand about four inches from the side of the halter, you can make minor adjustments to the horse's way of going without calling attention to the fact that you are correcting your horse. Coil the balance of the lead line neatly in your left hand. Never hold your left hand below your waist. Hold your right hand on the leather segment of the line just below the chain at the horse's halter height.

When you start your pattern and step off from the cone at a walk, your horse should move off *with you* at a brisk walk. You will lose points if you must tug or pull on the lead line to get him to move. If your horse lags behind or rushes in front of you, you will also lose points. *His throat latch should stay at your shoulder,* as if there is an invisible yardstick gluing the two of you together—his throat latch joined with your shoulder. By this time, you should no longer have to glance at your horse to see if he is coming with you. You must trust that you have taught him well and walk straight to the first cone without looking at your horse. This shows a great deal of confidence in your horse, and is correct.

A foot or two before the cone, stop the horse and go right into your 360-degree turn. Never do anything that the pattern does not call for. A hesitation here, unless specifically called for in the pattern, will cost you points in tough company. The judge wants to see you step right into the 360 turn.

The first step of the 360 begins with the horse's left front leg crossing over in *front* of the right front leg—*not behind it.* Use the momentum from your brisk walk to help the horse set his weight back over his hocks to make a brilliant, energetic, 360-degree turn. His right hind pivot foot should remain planted in the ground as his body, which

If the chain on your lead is too long, an emergency quick fix is to double it back and snap it to itself.

should remain straight from head to tail, rotates around his pivot foot. As you finish the turn, you should be in the exact same position as when you began. Don't overshoot your turn and stop too late or your next line will not be straight, and don't stop too soon or you will lose the flow of the 360.

Without hesitating from the 360, move right into a trot. Again, your horse should step off into the trot as if he and you are of the same mind. Shouting "trot" or clucking so loudly that it becomes a distraction is not acceptable. Ideally, your horse will have learned to trot from your nonverbal body language. A *slight* shift of your shoulders can cue him to walk or trot. Over time, you will be able to omit all verbal cues and clucks.

It takes time and practice for your horse to learn to cue off your body language and go directly into a trot. Your goal—the ultimate finished product—is a horse that will walk or trot alongside you with no verbal or obvious hand or lead-line signals from you. Ultimately, your horse will also understand when to stop from watching your body language and he will stop squarely from a trot.

Trot straight toward the judge. Look at the judge and not at your horse. Stop a few feet in front of the judge. You will lose many points if you force the judge to take a step back in fear of being bowled over by your overly exuberant horse.

As soon as your horse has stopped, turn and face him by taking a step forward with your left foot. Then pivot and bring your right foot in line with your left foot. Hopefully, your horse has stopped with at least his hind feet square, but in any case, use your lead-line

---

SOME HELPFUL PATTERN TIPS

∩   Walk the pattern without your horse as you say the maneuvers aloud. Physically turn in place as you say the words "360-degree turn," or actually back up five steps as you say "back up five steps," and so on.

∩   Draw the pattern on paper to help yourself remember it. Mark out the 360-degree turn, the line on which to back up, and the path that you will follow while both walking and trotting your horse.

∩   Watch another exhibitor perform the pattern first so that you understand exactly what is called for. Be careful, though, because if the first person makes a mistake, all the exhibitors that follow can make a mistake if they assume that the first exhibitor was correct. Read your pattern and ask questions if you are unsure.

∩   Always read the pattern two or three times.

∩   Observe the setup of the cones in the arena so that you can visualize the pattern and see where your horse must be in relation to them.

cues to tell him to set up. Once your horse is set in the proper square position, turn your head, look at the judge and nod. This tells him that you are ready for the inspection.

A judge spends many hours on his feet throughout the course of a typical show day, and most judges do not have much patience with a horse that doesn't set up quickly. It honestly does not take long to teach a horse to set up with a minimum of fuss, and this is something that you should practice long before you enter your first class.

During the inspection, your body, from your toes to your shoulders, should be pointed at the horse's right front foot. As the judge moves around the horse, use the quarter method to give him an unobstructed view of your horse at all times. Your body always points toward the horse and you only swivel your head to watch the judge. Remember to glance at your horse once or twice to be sure that he is holding position.

When the judge nods that he has finished the inspection, ask your horse to step right off into a 180 turn. A 180 turn is half of a 360 and is performed exactly the same for half of the maneuver. You just stop sooner (when you have swapped end for end). Look back at the judge to be sure that you are correctly in line with him, then step right off into the trot, picking a visual aid directly in front of you so that you travel in a straight path back to the lineup. Look back once at the judge as you are trotting to the lineup to be sure that you are still in a straight line with the judge directly behind you, and proceed past the other horses. Stop your

horse and go right into another 180-degree turn, then walk him forward into the lineup and set up once again. Glance at the judge to indicate that you have completed the pattern.

Although you have technically finished your pattern, you must still remain alert and keep an eye not only on your horse, but on the judge. If the judge moves down the line to the left of your horse after he has finished with all of the contestants, switch sides so that you are now on the right side of your horse, giving the judge an unobstructed view of him. If the judge changes sides again and goes to the right side of your horse, you must switch and move to the left side. Continue this "dance" until the end of the class.

Watch your horse so that he does not try to rest or cock a leg or get out of position. This is where the time that you spent at home prepares your horse for standing correctly for long periods. *The class is not over until the ribbons are handed out.*

When the announcer reads the list of winners, no matter what placing you receive, thank the ring steward and smile as you exit the ring. While you may or may not agree with how the class was placed, *the judge's decision is final.* At any given show, you are paying for a judge's opinion on that day. Yelling or causing a scene not only makes the judge remember you next time, but sets a bad example for children and even the spectators watching the class. Be a good sport, take whatever ribbon you receive, if any, and work on the mistakes you discovered as you prepare for the next show.

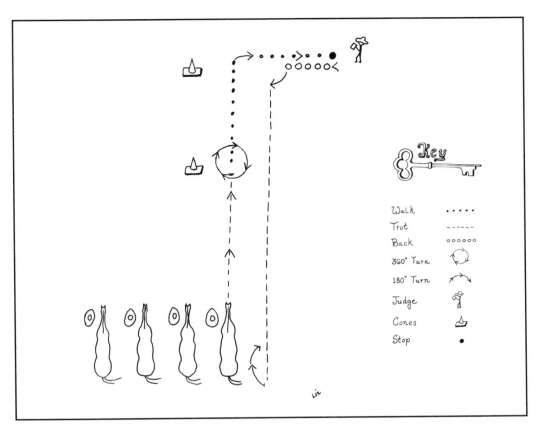

SAMPLE PATTERN TWO

Be ready and waiting so that when the contestant before you finishes his pattern, you do not make the judge wait for you to get into position. Step off into a brisk trot to the first cone. Use the momentum from that trot to step your horse right into the 360-degree turn in place. Walk briskly to the second cone. Stop with your horse's hip in line with the judge so that as you make the 90-degree turn, your horse will be able to travel in a straight line to the judge. Pivot to turn to face your horse, set him up, and nod to tell the judge that you are ready for the inspection.

Use the quarter method to follow the judge around the horse. Let the judge lead while you follow. Don't anticipate! Always give the judge an unobstructed view of your horse. Move briskly yet naturally from left to right. When the judge is finished and nods, move back to the left side if necessary, then back up exactly five steps. Go immediately into a ninety-degree or right turn and trot back to the lineup, looking at the judge once as you trot back. Trot through the lineup, stop, and go directly into the 180-degree turn. Walk back to your spot in the line up and set your horse up.

Pattern 3.

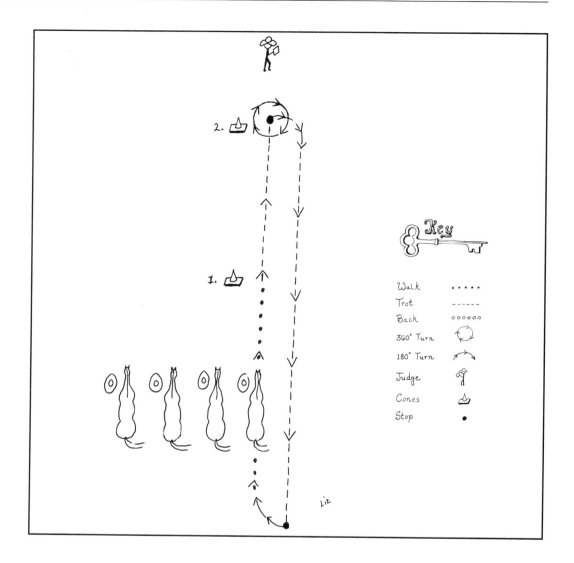

Walk   · · · ·
Trot   - - - - -
Back   ooooooo
360° Turn
180° Turn
Judge
Cones
Stop   ·

SAMPLE PATTERN THREE

Be ready so that when the judge nods for you to begin, you can step right off in a brisk walk to the first cone. Don't walk until the horse walks. Pulling on the lead line will cost you points, as will a horse that surges in front of you. Your horse should step off as you do. As your horse's front leg passes the first cone, go briskly into a trot. Look at the judge and smile as you travel straight at him. Be sure that you stop your horse about five or six feet in front of him. Never get so close that a judge feels like he must take a step backward or risk getting stepped on by your horse.

As your horse comes to a stop, use the momentum to go directly into the 360. Leaving those few extra feet in front of the judge when you stop should guarantee that you will not end up in the judge's lap as you finish the 360. Stop your horse after he does the 360 with your horse's head facing the judge, exactly straight on. Set him up in three seconds or less. Turn and face your horse with your toes pointing at your horse's right front foot, and turn only your head to look at the judge. This tells him that you are ready for the inspection.

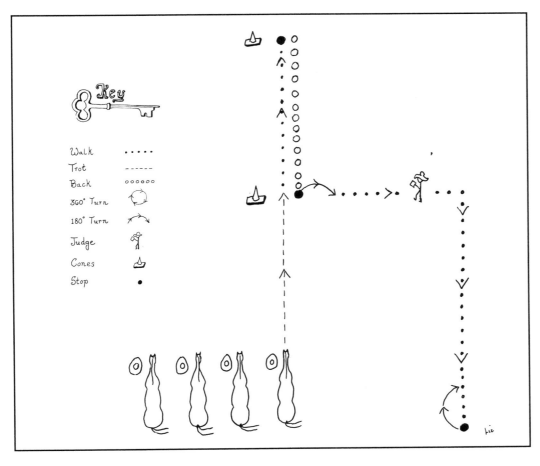

Pattern 4.

Use the quarter method as the judge performs the inspection. When he nods to release you, go directly into a 180-degree turn so that you are now headed back in the direction from which you came. Do not overshoot the mark where you are supposed to stop when performing the 180-degree turn, or you will have to travel a crooked path back to the line up, thus losing points. Look at the judge. Step right off into the trot, look back once again at the judge to be sure that he is still directly behind you, and go through the line up of horses to the fence. Do another 180-degree turn and reset your horse in his original position.

SAMPLE PATTERN FOUR

When the judge nods to begin, have your horse ready and waiting at the cone. Step briskly off into a trot to the first cone. Your horse should trot right off with you—with no visible cue from you! When his front leg reaches the first cone, your horse should return to a walk *from your walking steps.* Your horse should be so in tune with your body language that you do not have to pull back on the lead shank to make him walk. He should cue off your body language.

At the second cone, stop, pivot to face your horse, and ask him to back up until he reaches the first cone that you passed. The pattern calls for a ninety-degree turn before you walk to the judge to set up. You must plan where to stop so that your ninety-degree turn places you directly across from the judge. To do this, stop when your *horse's hip is in line with the judge.* In this way, when your horse plants his right hind pivot foot and pivots around it, keeping his body straight from head to tail, he will end up directly in line with the judge, allowing you to walk directly to the judge without curving your path and losing points. Set up for inspection. When the judge is finished, he'll nod to release you. Walk straight past the judge, still in the same direction as you were when you stopped, and return to the lineup.

HEAD TO TAIL OR SIDE TO SIDE LINEUP

A judge may ask you to line up either side-by-side or head-to-tail. In either situation, be sure not to crowd the exhibitor next to you. Give yourself plenty of room to maneuver. When you return to or go through the lineup after performing your pattern, be careful not to disturb the horses on either side.

When returning to the line in a side-by-side lineup, walk or jog (whichever the pattern calls for) quietly through the line of horses, stop, do a 180 degree turn in place, walk into the lineup and set your horse.

In a head-to-tail lineup, when you have finished your pattern, line up behind the horse in front of you and set your horse, allowing one horse length between exhibitors. Give yourself plenty of room, or follow the ring steward's direction. Remember to continue to "show" your horse until the class is over— and it isn't over until the placings are announced.

Practice both lineup positions at home, perhaps using some of your friend's horses to accustom your horse to having horses and their handlers on either side or in front and behind him. Teach your horse to hold a square position for some time in either lineup.

SUMMARY

Each of the patterns we have discussed combines many of the same maneuvers. They are simply varied in the order in which they are requested. Following the pattern exactly as it is written and performing

Allow one horse-length between horses when setting up in the head-to-tail formation.

Practice both line-ups at home so your horse is used to having horses on either side or in front and behind him. Teach him to stand squarely for quite some time in either situation.

the maneuvers with brilliance and finesse will gain you points, while dragging your horse along behind you will lose points. Remember that practice makes perfect. The more you practice, the better your performance will be. Don't dwell on the negatives before, during, or after the class. Instead, use your mistakes as guidelines for those areas requiring more practice. There's always another day, another judge, and another show. Just smile, enjoy yourself, and do your best.

SCHOOLING SHOWS

To ease the anxiety that always seems to be present at an exhibitor's first show, I suggest that you think of these first shows only as extended training. You've trained your horse at home, and now you must further his education at some small schooling shows. This will ease the stress that many competitors put on themselves and their horses. An added benefit is that it may help to keep your horse honest longer. Many horses learn quite early in life, that "anything goes" in the show ring because their handlers don't correct them at a show.

Pay the entry fee at a few smaller schooling shows, and use those shows to train your horse. Similarly, if a horse ever exhibits bad behavior, go back to the schooling shows and correct him just as you do at home. The cost of a schooling show or two is well worth the benefit gained. Just be sure that your corrections do not jeopardize another exhibitor, his horse or their performance, and thus interfere with his chance of winning a ribbon.

THINK POSITIVELY

Keep this thought foremost in your mind: if you think you can perform a pattern correctly, *you can.* If you think either you or your horse will mess up at a certain segment of the pattern, *you will mess up that segment of the pattern.* Be positive. Tell yourself, "Today is my lucky day and my horse will choose

Practice all the pattern maneuvers at home, and practice trotting in cadence with your horse.

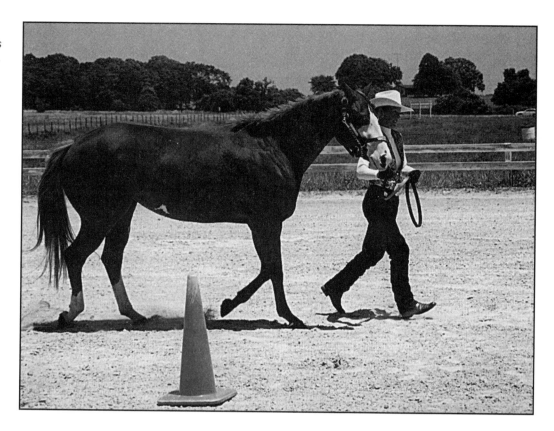

today to perform with brilliance. We can ace this pattern."

When the last call comes for your class, and it is almost your time to enter the arena, take one last look at your pattern or run through the pattern in your mind one more time. Banish any and all negative thoughts to the bottom of your manure pile back home, put a natural, friendly smile on your face, then enter the arena and do your best. This is when you will see the benefit of all those hours that you spent at home practicing. Your horse's throat latch will stay at your shoulder, he will perform the 180- or 360-degree turn with precision, he will set up in a matter of seconds, and he will back up as readily as he moves forward. When you leave the arena with the blue ribbon, you'll be glad you put your time in at home, practicing the showmanship maneuvers, and that you thought positive!

CHAPTER TEN

TIPS FOR ENHANCING THE PATTERNS

A poised, confident, neatly attired exhibitor.

THE RULES in the American Quarter Horse Association rule book say, "The ideal showmanship performance consists of a poised, confident, neatly attired exhibitor leading a well-groomed and conditioned horse that quickly and efficiently performs the requested pattern with promptness, smoothness, and precision." The judge must judge the class accordingly.

An exhibitor with a good self-carriage who stands up tall and looks the judge in the eye, who smiles naturally and carries himself with dignity and grace (not slouching or looking at the ground), will do well in this class. Your attitude shouts to the judge, without you ever saying a word, that you know your horse is able to perform whatever maneuvers may be asked of him and that you are proud to be showing him.

Attitude plays such a big part in showmanship that it can win the class for you or keep you completely out of the ribbons. You can have the best-trained horse in the class and perform the best pattern, but if you do not stand tall and show in a confident manner, you will knock yourself way down in the point

Two examples of unacceptable dress. They are fine for schooling at home but never for showing.

standings. If you lack confidence, you must work hard on gaining a better self-image in order to do well in this class. This is an easy class *to train a horse for,* but if you are not the type of person who carries himself with pride and confidence, the best-trained horse will not win this class for you.

Many people seem to think that the emphasis of this class is on the exactness of the pattern, and they forget that their attitude is a major segment of their score, and so is the condition and cleanliness of the horse.

Teach your horse to lead correctly beside you. Do not drag him by the lead line or let him rush in front of you. Do not lead him in an unnatural or overly animated manner. Do not bend over and lead your horse with your head and neck stuck out in front of you like a turtle trying to win a race by a head.

Stand up, be natural, and lead your horse in a poised and confident manner. Smile at the judge—a natural, pleasant smile, not one that is fake or overdone. Over-showing is as much a turn-off as is under-showing. The rules state: "Poise and confidence." Show with dignity, be

courteous, and be genuinely sportsmanlike.

BE APPROPRIATELY ATTIRED

Your attire does not seem to matter as much as showing your horse confidently, although, obviously, you wouldn't want to enter the arena wearing your barn clothes. I have seen exhibitors with starched jeans and a western shirt win a class over better-dressed competitors, especially at the smaller shows. They performed the pattern correctly, showed their horse to the best of their ability, and were rewarded for it. However, nice clothes in which you feel attractive often give you that little boost that adds to your confidence. The best advice that I can give you is to dress to the level of show in which you are participating, but be sure to wear clothes that are comfortable and that make you feel good about yourself. (See Chapter 5 for a more detailed discussion of clothing.)

CONDITION YOUR HORSE

If you want to catch the judge's eye, you must enter the arena with a well-groomed and conditioned horse. Conditioning and grooming start long before your first show. Although *you*, not your horse, are being judged, your ability to fit and show a halter horse is a big factor in the judge's decision. You would not expect to win at halter with a horse that you pulled out of the pasture on Saturday night for a show on Sunday with a raggedy hair coat and rolls of flab hanging under his belly. Well, you can't expect to win at showmanship either under these conditions. The rules specify a well-groomed and conditioned horse. While this class *is not* judged on your horse's conformation, it *is* judged on your ability to fit and condition a horse. You can make an average horse stand out from the crowd with good grooming and proper conditioning.

At higher levels of showmanship, a nicely portioned, well-balanced horse with that certain charisma will catch a judge's eye more than a plainer horse that is equally fit and groomed. While the rules specifically state that the horse's conformation is not being judged, a judge at the higher levels assumes that you know and understand the rules behind conformation—form to function—and would choose to own a well-conformed horse. A horse with a minor conformation flaw would not necessarily be out of the ribbons. However, if a horse has a number of flaws or one flaw that is glaringly obvious, it will make a difference at this level. The less eye-catching your horse is, the more you will have to work on his hair coat, conditioning, and performance to catch a judge's eye.

KNOW THE MANEUVERS

A horse must quickly and efficiently perform the requested maneuvers with precision and smoothness. *The only way to accomplish this is to spend time at home on the ground training your horse.* Much as you stumbled through your ABCs when you first learned them, so a horse will stumble though the showmanship maneuvers until they become second nature to him. Practice makes perfect. Some of the common mistakes while performing a pattern are caused more by handler error than by the horse actually misbehaving or not performing as he should. Plan to spend ten to fifteen minutes a day for ninety days working on the showmanship maneuvers, while also conditioning your horse, before your first show. Ninety days will give him the time to learn and understand what you are asking of him with each cue that you use.

SET UP QUICKLY

If your horse will not set up in approximately three seconds in the arena, expect to lose points. If it takes much longer than those three seconds, set him up to the best of your ability within that time frame and let the judge perform his inspection. Then go home and practice, practice, practice. A judge does not like to spend his time waiting for you to set up your horse. He expects that you have trained your horse beforehand.

You cannot touch a horse with your hands or legs (or toes) to set him up in a showmanship class. A judge expects that you have taught your horse to set up on cue, without physical help from you in the arena. The time to practice is at home, prior to entering your first class.

Making a judge wait unnecessarily as you push or pull your

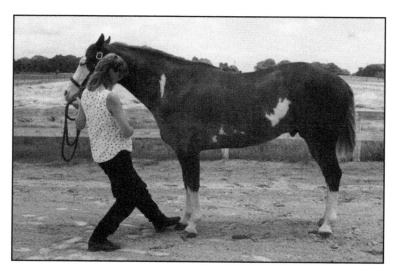

You cannot use your toe to move your horse's foot in a showmanship class. In a halter class it would be acceptable, although not preferred.

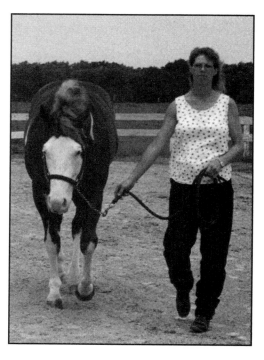

This handler is too far away, and she is using a chain that is too long.

horse back and forth to set him up leaves him with a bad image, and it will show in your score. If your horse won't set up, get him as close as you can, smile, and nod at the judge to tell him that you are ready to have him perform the inspection.

PRACTICE LEADING

Some handlers cause a horse to lose form when leading by holding the end of the lead line too close to the horse's head and tipping or pulling the horse's head to the left. When you do this, you prevent the horse from tracking straight. He will walk or jog with his body bent and his head tipped toward you. Hold the lead line three to four inches away from the horse's halter, and leave a slight loop in the chain so that your horse can travel in a straight line without interference.

Another very common handler error is stepping off too soon and dragging the horse behind. Give

This handler is too close to the horse and her hand is on the chain which is a serious offense. Never put your hand on the chain.

Do not pull the horse's head to you when you lead him. You must allow him to track in a straight line.

Ask your horse to step off. Then you walk off with him. Stay at his throat latch. Line up your right shoulder with the judge's right shoulder and your horse should then be lined up with the judge as you walk to him.

your horse a second to read your body language before stepping off at a walk or jog. Don't move until your horse does! Lead your horse in the same manner that you do at home. Don't change your routine because you are at a show. Your horse has become accustomed to your routine at home, and he will look for those cues. It is better to go a bit slower, yet perform the pattern with precision, than to rush through a pattern. While a judge might get aggravated by your horse taking too long to set up, he will allow you all the time you need to perform the pattern (provided, of course, that you don't drag it out to an extreme).

STAY IN POSITION

When leading your horse, be sure that you are even with his throat latch, not in front of it or behind it. Always lead from the left side.

In the event that you end up on the right side of the horse when the judge finishes his inspection and you need to either lead your horse back to the lineup or go on to perform another maneuver, first step back to the left side of the horse. Don't make it a big deal. Take your three steps to switch sides, as discussed in the quarter method of showing, and continue on with your pattern. A mistake, such as leading a horse from his right side, will keep you out of the ribbons no matter how well the rest of your pattern went.

READ YOUR PATTERN

When you look at a pattern, remember that when it calls for a straight line, the judge expects to see *a straight line*. If the pattern calls for an "S" or a curved line (from one cone to another), then he expects to see that same "S" or curved line. If the pattern calls for you to start at the left side of the first cone

Correctly backing a horse.

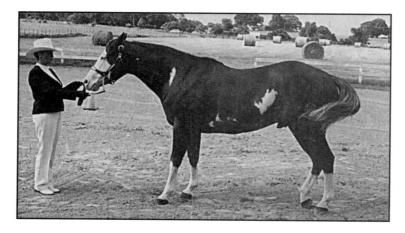

Bad! Bad! Bad! Out of square. A hoof resting. Standing in front of the horse. (That is dangerous!) All these are points off your score.

Stop with your horse's front leg at the cone. His body must stay aligned from head to tail.

and end at the right side of the last cone, then that is exactly what the judge is expecting to see. If the pattern calls for five steps back, then the judge wants you to count and back up *exactly* five steps. Read your pattern! If you're not sure you understand the pattern, ask questions before the class starts. Going even slightly off pattern in a showmanship class will affect your final score.

Tip: Any time a pattern specifies a specific number of steps, rest assured that the judge is a stickler for perfection and will count the number of steps that you make, and he will expect you to do the same.

MOVE SMOOTHLY

Another common mistake is when the handler pulls a horse around a turn (to the left), such as when you walk back to the lineup, rather than pushing the horse around the turn (to the right). Whenever you turn a horse, especially when turning in place to retrace your tracks, you must turn the horse to the right and move him away from you. This is for safety reasons. If you pulled the horse toward you, he could step on your toe, bump or slam into you, or he could jump and hit you. Always push a horse away from you when making a turn. Pivot to face the horse. Then ask him to turn using the same method as for a 180-degree.

When asking your horse to perform a 90- or 360-degree turn, first turn to your right. Face your horse's head, and step into the horse so that he moves away from you to the right.

When you ask the horse to back up, you must turn and face the rear of the horse. Walk forward

The horse's body must stay aligned from head to tail.

This horse's head is turned to the right, and is not in alignment with his body.

while the horse walks backward. This is something that you should work on at home, because your horse will probably not understand the first time or two that you ask.

MAKE STRAIGHT STOPS

When you ask your horse to stop, he must remain with his body in a straight line. He should not throw his hip to the left or to the right. A horse that has not been schooled in these maneuvers will often stop crooked. You must teach him that when you stop, he stops. He cannot twist or turn. He must remain straight throughout his entire body until you give him the next cue to perform. In time, he'll learn to stop squarely provided that you let him know a stop is coming.

CREATE A SEAMLESS PERFORMANCE

Mostly, the showmanship class is based on a safe, efficient, well-performed pattern by a horse-and-handler team that has practiced the maneuvers so that they tie together and appear seamless. Look at the experience of each show as a report card of your training time spent at home. If your "grade" was not as high as you would have liked it to be, you will have to go home and study or practice more. There's always another show, another report card, another day. Learn from your mistakes. Most of all, enjoy the time that you spend with your horse teaching him to be more mannerly on the ground. This will also help you with the showmanship maneuvers.

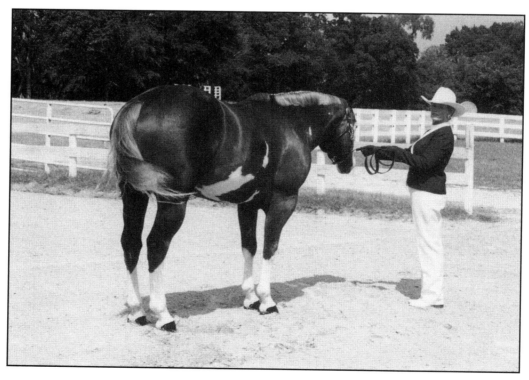

Stop your horse squarely with his body in a straight line. Remember: "practice makes perfect."

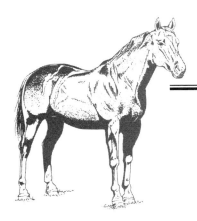

CHAPTER ELEVEN

CONDITIONING YOUR HORSE

GOOD GROOMING, proper feed, and a good worm-control program, combined with the proper conditioning program, will all contribute to a winning look that is so important in showmanship. Everything else being equal, the horse with glistening hair coat and a shining body with rippling muscles will win. As the rules state, the horse is only a "prop," but nevertheless you are judged on your ability to fit and prepare your horse for competition. A properly groomed and conditioned horse shows that you have done your homework and that you have prepared your horse to his maximum potential.

THAT WINNING LOOK

Another reason to make your horse look positively outstanding is that you will feel good about him, and *that* will show in your attitude. You can beat a superbly turned-out horse if the handler does not present his horse well. But, if two handlers have the same showing or handling ability, the better-groomed and conditioned horse will win the class. To quote the rule book, "The horse's body condition and overall fitness should be assessed." The Quarter Horse rules give ten out of a possible twenty points to the appearance of the exhibitor and the *physical appearance of the horse.* So, if you want to win, go the extra mile and make your horse look his absolute best. His actual conformation may not be the best in the class, but his condition and coat should be the absolute best that you are capable of making them.

Clean water, whether it comes from a pond, a stream, a bucket, or an automatic waterer, is essential for horses to live.

FIVE FACTORS FOR SUCCESS

The five factors involved in making your showmanship horse look his absolute best are:

Feeding
Worming
Vaccinations
Trimming or shoeing
Conditioning

DIET

A horse must be on a good diet to look his best. While different feeds are used across the country, your feed supplier or veterinarian should be able to help you determine a balanced diet that is just right for your horse.

I feed a Pilgrims Pride® 12-percent pellet feed with a 4 1/2-half percent fat content to every horse older than two, and every horse in my barn has a bloom to his coat that is simply amazing—without any supplements. I keep my horses wormed and their stalls and pens clean, and offer good-quality hay and fresh water. They are stalled in the heat of the day to avoid sun bleaching of their coat and are let out late at night, with the stallions staying out all night. I do not like to keep a horse locked in a stall without turnout time. The turnout time makes them happier and more easy to manage. While your showmanship horse will probably not be a stallion—I recommend against it—these same guidelines can be applied to any horse.

Keep in mind that you cannot toss musty old hay to your horse and expect him to look his best. Old, musty hay can cause respiratory problems, a cough, colic, and in general make your horse look "poor."

He will not get the best possible nutrients—fat, protein, minerals, vitamins, and fiber—from poor-quality feed. As with any athlete, a horse must eat the best to look his best. Good feed, a good worming program and a safe, clean environment are all important measures when conditioning a horse.

To Grain or Not to Grain?

On the same note, not all horses require a lot of grain. Grain should be added to the horse's diet if he cannot maintain his weight on good-quality hay or pasture alone. Most horses that are worked hard need the extra help from grain, but do not feed an overabundance of grain if your horse needs only a little. Some horses need grain to supplement their hay ration so that they can remain at the proper weight with a sparkling hair coat and good hoof quality.

Other horses, kept on good pasture, do not need grain. Adding grain to their diet would make them obese, which is not only unattractive, but unhealthy. Horses that have a large hay belly might be better off with a little grain added to their diet and a corresponding decrease in the amount of hay being fed. Feeding is often more an art than a science. Use the recommendations from your vet or on the feed labels as a guideline, and adjust the amount when you feel it is necessary. You are the best judge of what your horse needs to eat. Take a good look at his weight level every day or two, with the goal of keeping him at his optimum weight—not obese and not poor.

My personal preference is to feed more hay than grain as long as the horse maintains his weight and does not get a large hay belly. Here in Texas I feed properly fertilized coastal Bermuda hay along with the pelleted feed mentioned above. The high fat content keeps the hair coat sparkling, without added supplements, thus saving money. If your horse doesn't need supplements, don't waste your money. A lower protein diet also keeps a horse from getting too "high" so he can be handled with less fuss.

I feed horses younger than two years of age a 16-percent protein mix to help them grow properly and gain the maximum potential from the feed—without pushing to get them overweight or grow faster than their bones can support.

Because I start a lot of colts under saddle, I do not want them to be "high" from too much grain or protein. As one vet said, horses' joints only have so many moves in them. Anytime you have to work a colt down for two hours before you can begin to teach him anything, you are also wearing out his joints.

There are almost as many theories on feeding horses as there are ways to ride and train them. I can only tell you the method that I use and have had success with. If a horse looks, acts, and feels good, leave his feed as it is. If one is losing weight, first have his teeth checked for abnormalities. Then do a fecal analysis to be sure that worms are not the cause of the weight loss. Once you have the results of those two items, you can add feed to increase his weight, worm him if necessary, or in some way make a change that benefits him.

Salt and Minerals

A horse needs salt and minerals year-round, but especially in the summer when he sweats from being worked in the heat. Some horses need added electrolytes to keep them in balance. Horses lose salt by sweating, just as we do, and salt is a very real requirement of all living things. If the grain that you use does not have minerals in it, offer a mineral block free choice, or add minerals directly to the feed. Your horse will feel better and stay healthier with the correct ration of minerals and salt.

Clean, Fresh Water

Every horse needs clean, fresh water in front of him at all times! Lack of water is a big cause of colic. If a horse doesn't drink enough water, or doesn't drink enough water to replace what he loses by sweating, he can dehydrate or impact and colic.

In the northern states, warming a horse's water in the winter will encourage him to drink more. Offer warmed water at least twice a day. If your horse has a history of colic in the winter, warming his water is one way to help avoid this problem. I saw the water intake of horses in Connecticut almost double when I began to offer warmed water twice a day. The horses that had a history of colic ceased to colic in the winter. Horses do not like ice-cold water, just as we do not when it is ten degrees and frigid outside.

You ensure your horse's good health when you spend extra money on quality hay and offering

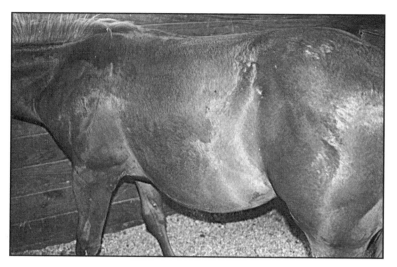

The bloated look to this five-month-old colt's belly suggests a worm problem. Start your colts on a good worming program and continue throughout his lifetime.

Three to five days after worming, these lung worms were found in his manure. Worms can cause serious internal problems, as well as the dull coat and bloated belly of the colt at the left.

fresh, clean water at all times. Remember—you want the healthiest horse, carrying the correct amount of weight for his frame, with the best hair coat possible. A good hair coat starts on the inside and is polished on the outside with proper grooming.

WORMS

Starting on the inside includes keeping your horse on a regular worming program. Freedom from worms is necessary for your horse to maximize the feed he receives. In simple terms, if your horse is wormy, the worms will steal the nutrients that your horse should be getting from his feed. You will save money, *and the horse's overall health will be better* in the long run, by keeping him on a good worming program. Follow your veterinarian's recommendations. You can use one of the daily wormers or a paste wormer every two months. I've begun using Quest® as my wormer of choice. Because it is new, the worms have not had time to build

up a resistance to the drug in it. I worm my horses every two months as a rule. If a horse comes into my barn looking wormy, I worm him with strongid once a month, or twenty days apart if the problem is caused by strongyles. The life cycle of strongyles is twenty-one days. Waiting longer than twenty days to worm the second time allows a new batch of worms to hatch, and then those worms begin to breed. Break the cycle by worming within twenty days when a fecal analysis reveals a strongyle problem.

Keeping your stalls and paddocks clean will help keep the worm infestation to a minimum. If you keep the manure, and therefore any worms that may be in the manure, out of the stalls and paddocks, the horse cannot re-ingest the worm eggs that would continue the cycle. I also lime my stalls daily to help avoid thrush and white line disease. A fecal analysis done once or twice a year is a cheap and effective way to see if your worming program is on the right track. Don't try to save money by buying the cheapest

This is a bot fly. They hover around the horse looking for a place to lay their eggs. The horse licks the eggs and ingests them into his system where they hatch and become worms.

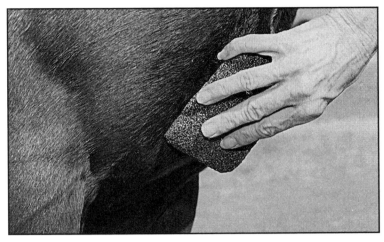

Remove the bot fly eggs with a bot block or a razor or bot fly knife. The tiny white specks below the bot block are bot fly eggs, golden in color. Worm for bots with ivermectin in the fall after a hard frost.

wormers—they just don't do the job. Check with your veterinarian about the best worming program for your area and your horse. Worming saves you money in the long run by lowering your feed bill, and it preserves your horse's good health.

A good worming program would also help to avoid many of the colic cases seen today. A wormy horse often has a potbellied, rough-hair-coated appearance. He will not shed out as easily as his worm-free cousins, and he will not have the type of hair coat that you need to win at showmanship. He will not gain or hold his weight, and he will not have that bloom to his coat. Have a fecal analysis done so you know exactly what type of worm you are dealing and can use the appropriate drug to treat it.

VACCINATIONS

In addition to a good worming schedule, keeping your horse on a regular vaccination schedule is important. You wouldn't want to wake up the day before a very im-portant show (or any show, for that matter) to find your horse with a runny nose and cough. Most rhino-flu vaccines are effective for only two to three months. Therefore, they must be given more than once or twice a year to keep your horse actively immune from whatever current strains are going around.

I also vaccinate for Eastern Encephalomyelitis (EEE), Western Encephalomyelitis (WEE) and Venezuelan Encephalomyelitis (VEE). A tetanus vaccination is always good insurance—you never know when your horse might get cut or step on something like a rusty nail. The cost of a shot is cheap insurance. I keep a spare vaccine on hand in the event that a horse should get cut so I can give a booster—just in case.

In Connecticut, I vaccinated for Potomac Horse Fever after seeing two cases nearby and hearing of many others. In Texas it is not prevalent, so I have not vaccinated for it. Ask your vet and follow his recommendations for your area. Remember that while a yearly booster is sufficient for most diseases, a booster of rhino-flu should be given every two to three months, at least during the busy show season.

FIND A QUALIFIED FARRIER

Another important factor that will help keep your horse sound is to employ a qualified farrier and schedule successive visits every five to seven weeks—sooner if your horse needs it, as he might in the summer. A horse's hooves do not grow as fast in the winter, so you may be able to go a bit longer between visits during that time of year. Discuss this with your farrier. Horses use the keratin from a balanced diet to grow hooves and hair. In the winter, keratin is used to produce the long winter coat, which keeps horses warm if they are left unblanketed. Therefore, they grow more hair than hoof.

Your horse needs to be trimmed or shod *on a regular basis* in order to travel correctly. Properly trimmed or shod hooves allow a horse to work and not come up sore. Overly long toes, shoes that are loose or falling

off, or hooves that are out of balance will all cause a faulty gait. A horse must be comfortable in order to work at his maximum potential. Horses with overly long hooves will trip and stumble, or overreach (hit the back of a front fetlock with a hind shoe). They also might forge (not quite as severe), hitting the toe of a front shoe with the toe of a hind shoe, or they could strain a tendon or ligament because of incorrect angles. Any of the above can cause unsoundness.

When I was a child, my showmanship horse tripped over a rock that I did not see. That stumble cost me the class. The judge said that I should have picked a better path so that the horse didn't stumble. A *rock caused that horse* to stumble, but overly long or improperly trimmed or shod horses will trip or stumble on level, even ground. Tripping or stumbling create flaws in an otherwise seamless presentation.

Before hiring a new farrier, ask for recommendations from your vet. While your friends may *like* him, go beyond his personality. Rather than ask, "How do you like him and how long do your horse's shoes stay on?" ask, "How sound does your horse travel?" I'd rather have a horse lose a shoe and pay to have it reset than have a horse pull a large chunk of hoof off because of overly long clinches from a farrier who wanted to make sure that the shoes stay on.

Check to see if your horse's shoulder angles match his pastern angles, which should match his hoof angles. Leaving a long toe and short heel on a Quarter Horse is asking for unsoundness problems down the road. This type of shoeing makes a horse look as if he is walking on skis. As his feet begin to grow, his toes will begin to shoot upward. You

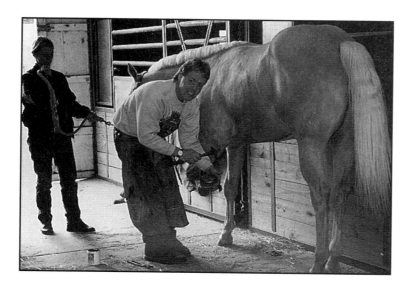

Find a good farrier. This is my son, Don Truskauskas.

might also notice the horse slapping the ground in front with his front feet as he lopes or canters.

As a general rule, a Quarter Horse's front hooves should measure approximately three and one-quarter inches from the bottom of his toe to the hairline of his coronet band. His hind hooves should measure three and one-half inches from the end of his toe to the hair line of his coronary band. While not every horse will match this exactly, if your horse is way off in his measurements, it is time to have him reshod or trimmed. If he was recently shod, it is time to ask your farrier why your horse is shod as he is. If your farrier cannot give you a straightforward answer, call your vet and discuss the issue. You may even want to bring the horse in for your vet to examine the shoeing job. (**Note:** If you show a horse of a different type than a Quarter Horse or Paint, he will be shod a bit differently. In that case, you must ask questions of someone familiar with your breed.)

While some farriers hate to be questioned about their work (they assume that they are qualified to shoe in the manner to which they have become accustomed), it is your horse and you have the right to ask questions. Many farriers especially hate for a person who is new to horses to ask questions about something they have read in a book. But, if you find that your horse is not traveling the way he should—after you have received a professional opinion from your vet or a professional trainer—you have the right to ask questions and should receive courteous answers.

Always remember—you want the most qualified farrier, not necessarily the nicest or cheapest farrier. Try to find a farrier who regularly handles the type of horse that you own. Quarter Horses are shod differently than Thoroughbreds, as are Arabians and Tennessee Walkers. Barrel horses are shod differently than western pleasure horses, and halter and showmanship horses might be shod a bit differently than their roping-horse cousins. There is an art to shoeing each type of horse correctly. It is your job to choose a farrier who shoes the type of horse that you own and plan to show.

Please note that a farrier has bills to pay and many other horses to care for. Calling him at midnight to ask him to come the next day because your horse lost a shoe—when your horse was last shod three months ago—is not likely to make you his best friend. In addition, teach your horse to stand quietly and to pick up his feet as part of his training program. He must learn to stand for showmanship; add a few minutes a day to teach him to *pick up* his feet. The farrier is *not* the trainer. It is *not his job* to teach your horse to pick up his feet. That is your job, or else it is your job to send your horse to a trainer who can teach him. Your farrier should not be expected to come to your house, catch your rank two-year-old in the pasture, teach him to pick up his feet (which obviously would take more than one day anyway), and trim your horse's hooves for twenty dollars while he risks his life or limb.

Clean your horse's feet daily as part of your grooming routine. This will help to prevent thrush and white line disease. It will also help teach your horse to have his feet handled. And it will help your farrier, whose job it is to be sure that your horse's hooves are trimmed or shod correctly so that your horse can have a long, successful, sound career.

If your horse's feet are excessively dry, your farrier (or your vet), may recommend the use of a hoof dressing or perhaps standing the horse in water or mud. There are, once again, many conflicting opinions on wet and dry feet. You do not want a horse's feet to become very soft and spongy, nor do you want them hard and brittle. You do not want them hard as a rock one day and soft and spongy the next. Ask your farrier for his recommendation. I use a hoof dressing two or three times a week, plus Koppertox® once a week, as a preventive measure for thrush and white line disease. Be sure that when you use a hoof dressing, you apply it to the underside of the hoof and the frog. Then move to the outside of the hoof, cover the entire hoof wall, and apply it a half inch up into the coronary band. Just don't do as I did when I was young child—I covered my horse's hooves with gooey hoof dressing just minutes before the farrier came, wanting him to think that I took really good care of my horse's hooves. Needless to say, he was not happy with me. His hands were covered with hoof dressing and the hooves slid right out of his hand.

If your horse spends a lot of time in a stall bedded with shavings or sawdust, that same bedding can easily draw the moisture right out of his hooves. Follow your farrier's recommendation on how to best care for your horse's feet. Extremely brittle hooves will not hold a shoe. Unshod brittle hooves are more prone to cracking and chipping. If your horse does not hold a shoe or grow new hoof as quickly as he should, you might try to supple-ment his diet with one of the commercial supplements available.

However, if you plan to add a supplement to your horse's diet, read the label carefully. Some products make claims that are not substantiated. Look at the content and try to get as much of what you need at the best possible price. For example, looking at a recent catalogue, one hoof supplement is priced at $15 for six pounds, while another product that weighs seven pounds costs $42. The difference? The first has 100 milligrams of biotin. The second has 800 milligrams per pound. Which is the better buy? The second. Eight times $15 is much more than $42. Do your homework before you buy.

Do not expect a farrier to perform miracles. Given enough time, many farriers can help a problem horse or one plagued with unsoundness problems, at least to a degree. The earlier a colt or young horse is started on a corrective trimming or shoeing program, the better your chances are to have a straight-legged horse. A straight-legged horse is not only more pleasing to watch from a judge's point of view, he is more likely to stay sound through a long and sometimes demanding career. While a showmanship judge should not knock you down for a crooked-legged horse, in tough or close competition, the little extra gained by leading a correct horse may give you the winning edge.

DON'T FORGET THE BOOTS

I use front splint boots on every horse that I work, whether riding, longeing, or ponying, just in case a horse hits himself with the opposing leg. In the long run, it is cheap insurance. I have been lucky to have had very few leg injuries caused by working a horse, and I credit that to always using protective leg gear. It not only keeps a horse from hitting one leg with another, it also gives him added support. This is especially important when you first start a horse to work in a conditioning program.

CONDITIONING PROGRAM

An out-of-condition horse is similar to a person who works at an office job all week and goes out to play four hours of tennis on a weekend. The next morning he wakes up so stiff and sore that he can barely move. A horse that is lucky enough to have some turnout time will be in slightly better shape than a horse that is stalled continuously. Still, they both need long, slow miles to bring them up to the proper condition. A pastured horse will walk about twenty miles a day in search of food. But he is still not putting in all-out effort to increase his muscle tone. He is simply walking to find food. A stalled horse obviously does not have that option. His hay and grain are placed in a feeder right in front of him, and he stands in one spot and munches. With either horse, you must begin by asking him to walk, and then to trot, for only a few minutes at a time. Slowly increase the amount of effort that he expends until he is able to handle the demands that you place upon him.

If you are taking a young horse, such as a two-year-old that has never been worked, or an older horse that has been standing idle for some time, expect to spend a minimum of forty-five to sixty days before he is conditioned so that he will present a pleasing, muscled-up

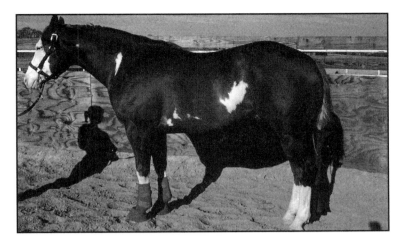

I always use splint boots to protect horses' legs, young and old alike, from an accidental bump.

From this...

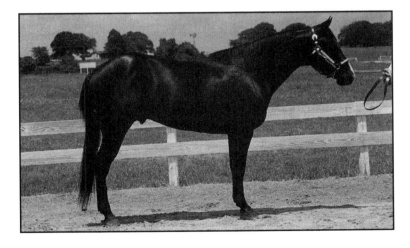

...to this in ninety days. Proper care and conditioning make a horse look good! Dangerous Devil Dan, a Quarter Horse stallion.

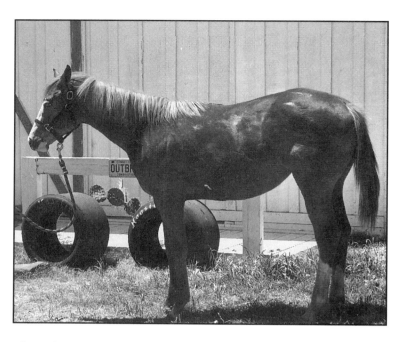

Sometimes you find a diamond in the rough (and priced accordingly).

From the photo above to this. . .

picture. At the end of ninety days, he should have good muscle tone and look well conditioned if you work him for twenty to thirty minutes a day, at least four times a week. A rule of thumb is, for every day you give a horse off, it takes that long to bring him back to his previous fitness level. For instance, if you turned your horse out to pasture for thirty days, it will probably take thirty days to bring him back to his prior fitness level. While some time off is certainly good for your horse's mental state of mind, too much time off is detrimental to his fitness. A horse seems to come back fresher after a brief period of rest, and this is certainly true if you have been campaigning your horse hard. Yet, you must plan his time off so you allow the necessary time to bring him back into condition before his next show.

A showmanship horse must be sleek and shiny; fit, not fat. A fat, out-of-condition horse is not attractive for showmanship and this will count against you. You can't leave conditioning until the last minute. Nor can you expect that fit condition to stay once you have reached the optimum level unless you continue to exercise your horse. The good news is, a fit and worm-free horse is much healthier than a fat, out-of-shape horse.

START SLOWLY

A horse must be brought *slowly* into shape so that his legs—the tendons, ligaments, and muscles—do not become overly stressed. If you are using this horse strictly for showmanship (or halter) and are not riding him, you must either longe him, put him in a round pen and free-longe him, or pony him.

Longeing is basically teaching a horse to move around you in a circle, either free-longeing in a round pen or on a line. Once your horse understands how to longe, begin by walking him for two to three minutes to get his muscles loosened and warmed up. *Whether you longe or ride, you should always start out by walking to warm a horse up and end by walking to cool him down.* Another benefit of teaching a horse to walk for the first few minutes of longeing is that he will not take off in a dead run as soon as he walks into the longeing area. Teach good manners right from the start.

After walking the horse for a few minutes, you may progress to trotting. If your horse is heavy or really out of shape and you notice him blowing or hear his breathing becoming labored, bring him back to a walk for a few minutes so that he can catch his breath. Then trot again. Halfway through, reverse sides and work him in the opposite direction. Start out with fifteen to twenty minutes of walking and trotting—about ten minutes per side. When the horse is able to maintain the trot for longer periods of time, increase the trotting time and decrease the amount of walking time. Usually, after two weeks the horse can maintain a slow, easy trot for ten to fifteen minutes out of the total twenty. By the third or fourth week, walk the horse only to cool him down or for the initial walking warmup. If you work your horse four to five times per week,

. . .to this! (Mature and in show condition at age three.)

you should begin to see some results of conditioning at the end of thirty days. The horse should have lost his belly and begun to look presentable. It will take another thirty, or even sixty, days before you can see muscle development.

Remember, some horses are genetically programmed to carry more muscle than others. For example, most halter horses today are big and bulky with bulging forearm, hind-end and gaskin muscles. A performance horse does not carry that kind of bulk, nor should you expect him to. You cannot put muscle where there is none to start. You can only enhance the muscle that a horse already has.

After you have finished longeing the horse, ask him to back up. Backing helps to develop gaskin muscles, both inside and outside the hind leg. And, since your horse will also need to back in many showmanship patterns, you are simultaneously developing his muscles and teaching him to back up readily on a lead line. I ask a horse to back up twenty to thirty feet the first day, then add about ten feet every day. At the end of two months, I have the horse backing two to three times around my arena, which is deep sand that increases the benefits (as long as it is not done to extremes). Back your horse after working him, when his muscles are broken down from the prior work and he will gain the most benefit from this exercise. Make him back up continuously, not just a few feet. Backing must be a sustained effort in order to give his muscles the maximum results. Another benefit of backing your horse *after* you have worked him is that he will be in no hurry to end his lesson. Rather than think, "Oh boy!

I want to finish so that I can go to my stall!" he thinks, "Gees. When I get done here, I have to back up all the way around that arena three times. I'm in no hurry to do *that!*"

Another rear muscle-building exercise you can do when free-longeing a horse in a round pen is to ask for a roll back *into the fence*. This means that you step in front of the horse as he is walking or jogging around the round pen—without saying "whoa!"—and extend your whip in front of him to cause him reverse his forward motion and send him in the opposite direction. (Never try this if your horse is galloping madly around the pen— somebody will get hurt.) The closeness to the fence will naturally cause the horse to lift his forehand as he rolls back and over his inside hock. You will see his inside hind leg extend up underneath himself as he lifts his front end up and around to make the turn. This exercise makes the horse really use his hind end and will therefore develop his muscles. Remember that this is hard work for a horse. Don't overdo it, especially if your horse is not yet fit or conditioned. Work him in both directions equally so that one side does not develop more than the other.

COOLING DOWN

After longeing and backing up, work on the showmanship maneuvers while the horse finishes cooling down. Let his breathing, pulse, and respiratory rates return to normal. When a horse's breathing rate returns to close to normal after three or four minutes, you know he is fit. Count the number of breaths that he takes in fifteen seconds, and multiply that by four to get the number per minute. His breathing should return to fifteen or sixteen breaths per minute.

If your horse seems unable to handle the demands of the fitness program you have mapped out, add more walking time and decrease trotting time until he seems able to handle more. Then, slowly decrease the walking time and add to the trotting time. Walking a horse will seldom create problems unless you carry it to extremes and ask him to walk for four hours the first time out. It is when you ask an unfit horse to extend his trot, canter, or lope for twenty to thirty minutes at a stretch that you run into problems. Use care, and watch what your horse is telling you. Don't ask him to overexert in the initial stages. Conditioning takes time, and you must allow your horse that time before expecting him to handle the demands of your conditioning program.

PULSE AND RESPIRATION

Know how he acts when he is healthy, and learn to observe signs of overwork or fatigue. One way to measure fitness is with his pulse. Endurance riders do this, especially when competing in 25-, 50-, or 100-mile rides. While your showmanship horse will not be put to that kind of test, you can borrow the fitness information that endurance riders have gained over the years. Take your horse's pulse at rest. Place your fingertips inside under the jawbone, or on the back and inside of his fetlock. Count the number of beats for fifteen seconds. Multiply that number by four to give you a reading per minute. After working your horse for a few minutes, stop your horse or let him walk and see how quickly he re-

turns to his original level. As he gains in condition, he should return to that pre-work level more and more quickly.

If you are worried that you have overdone the conditioning on a given day, check your horse's heart rate. It should be twenty-four to thirty-six beats per minutes. His temperature is another indicator and should be 99.5°F to 100.5°F. His breathing or respiratory rate should be twelve to sixteen breaths per minute. Be sure that your horse is standing alertly, not with his head hanging to the ground in exhaustion or from being overheated.

WATER AND BATHS

When your horse has cooled down and is breathing somewhat normally, he can be given some water. Never allow a hot horse to have ice-cold water. I almost always hose or rinse my horses in the summer to remove sweat and salt. If sweat dries it can make the horse rub from itchiness and thus ruin his hair coat. A horse can rub off chunks of his mane, tail, or body hair. Use warm water to rinse the horse and give him a few sips of warm, not ice-cold, water.

Hosing the large veins under the horse's neck and down the insides of his legs until he returns to more normal pulse and respiratory rates will help to cool a horse. Then rinse the rest of his body after he has cooled down.

Many horses learn to love baths in the summer. Hosing after every workout when your horse sweats will help to keep him clean. He doesn't need a full bath every time you work him—hosing will rinse him clean and help cool him. If all you have available is cold water, fill a bucket with water before you begin to work your horse and place it in the sun. This will warm up the water while you work the horse.

You cannot force a horse into condition. It happens gradually over a period of weeks, not days. Just keep at it and you will see your horse begin to blossom. If you are conditioning a horse that you are also riding, the method is similar, but you will be on his back rather than at the end of a longe line. Start slowly with some easy, long walks, and slowly add trotting, cantering or loping. Watch his respiratory and pulse rates and do not push for too much in the initial stages. Conditioning takes time. There are no shortcuts.

CHAPTER TWELVE

CLIPPING YOUR HORSE'S FACE AND LEGS

A GOOD CLIPPING JOB can greatly enhance a horse's face and overall appearance. It takes time and practice to learn how to clip neatly, so some practice sessions are in order before the first show. The good news is that a horse's hair will grow back. Any mistakes made during practice will grow back, allowing you to re-clip correctly the next time, once you've mastered the proper technique.

Clip your horse two to three days before a show. That little bit of time will allow a horse's hair to grow in so that the clipper tracks fade and the color where the hair was shaved blends, avoiding that just-clipped appearance. A quick touchup the night before or morning of the show might be needed on the muzzle whiskers; these can be touched up with an ordinary disposable razor.

I use the Oster A-5 clippers with a two-speed motor and have had good success with that model. A number-ten blade is a good all-purpose blade, while the number-forty blade cuts closer, more like a surgical cut, and is used on the ears, the muzzle, around the eyes, and under the jaw and throat latch. I use the number-ten blade on the bridle path, pasterns and up the legs. It is difficult to get a correct trim without the right tools or, in this case, the right size blades. These blades can be sharpened for about five dollars each, so you do not need to replace them.

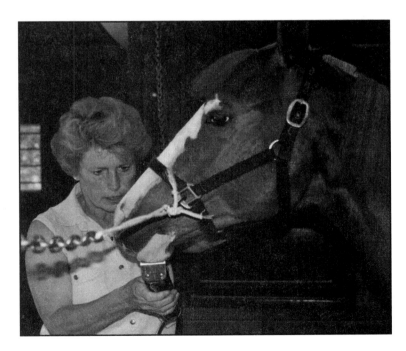

Start by clipping the face.

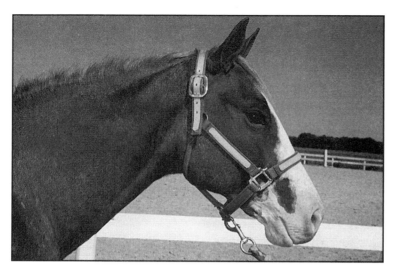

Before a bridle path is clipped.

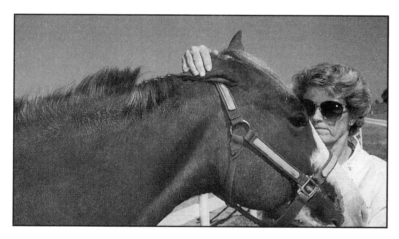

To get the correct length of the bridle path, lay his ear back. Clip to the end of his ear.

A finished bridle path.

INTRODUCE THE CLIPPERS SLOWLY

Most horses need to be introduced slowly to the clippers. At least a month before the first show start to accustom your horse to the clippers so that when the time comes for the show clip, he will be accepting of the clippers, allowing you to do a better job. In a pinch, a horse can be tranquilized a week before a show so that you can clip him. Remember, never use a tranquilizer right before the show or traces of it will show in his blood if a test is done. A twitch is another emergency measure, but unless the horse will stand without the twitch to allow you to clip his muzzle, you'll still be in for a fight getting those last hairs off his muzzle. The best and most successful clipping method is to train your horse to accept clippers readily.

I use a five-day program that in most cases teaches all but the very hardest horse to accept clippers. The first day, rub the clippers around the horse's head or as close as he will let you get them. When he stands reasonably quiet, praise him and put the clippers away.

The second day, you should be able to get a bit closer to the horse and perhaps clip a small section or two. Don't rush to get the final clipping job done. Just clip a little section if he will let you. Then rub his neck and put him up or work on something else.

The third day, take out your clippers again. You should be able to get still closer and can perhaps trim some of the long hairs under his chin or bridle path. Some horses will let you complete those areas; others will need more time. Take what your horse will give and repeat the process the next day. Remember, you are *introducing* clippers, not looking to get the finished trim.

Repeat this process on the fourth and fifth days. By the fifth day of this slow, easy, introductory method, your horse should stand easily for clipping. If not, continue with the program until he will let you clip him. Never put the clippers away when the horse is fighting you, or has thrown a fit, reared, pulled back, or broken a cross tie. Always wait for him to show his acceptance of the clippers at some stage before putting them away.

CLIPPING THE HORSE THAT HAS BEEN TRAINED TO STAND

Before you start, be sure that your blades are sharp. Dull blades will grab hair and pull or pinch, making your horse sure to be less cooperative the next time, especially in the sensitive ear, eye, or muzzle areas. Have blade wash and clipper lube on hand to keep blades cool and lubricated. Hot blades can burn a horse and are sure to make him hesitant to be clipped the next time. Hot blades do not clip as well as cool blades, and they leave more clipper marks.

Wash your horse and let him dry prior to clipping. A dirty horse will dull your blades more quickly than a horse that is clean and dry. Brush any loose hairs off, and keep a small brush handy for whisking away the loose hair after you have finished clipping so that you can see if you have missed any hairs. A stool is handy to enable you to reach the high spots, especially the bridle path and ears, if you are short or your horse raises his head.

Once your equipment is gathered, you're ready to begin. Start with the bridle path, using a number-ten blade. Push the horse's ear back flat against his neck to measure the length of the bridle path. The accepted method for a Quarter Horse or Paint is to cut the bridle path the length of the ear. Check your breed rules to determine the accepted length if you show another breed.

Once the bridle path is clipped from the bump or knob between the ears to the length of the ear, take your clippers and run them horizontally down the edges of the bridle path. This will blend in the remaining body hairs if some of them sticks up after you have clipped the mane.

If you clip your horse between shows, do not go to the end of the bridle path. Clip to within a half inch from the end of the bridle path and leave the rest alone. If you clip

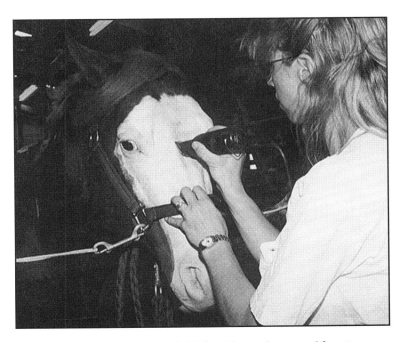

Clipping the white hairs on a bald-faced horse (or one with a star, strip, or snip) gives the head a neat, chiseled appearance.

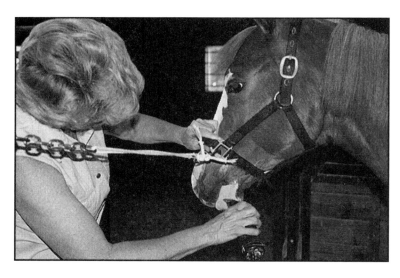

Clip under the jaw area and remove any long hairs.

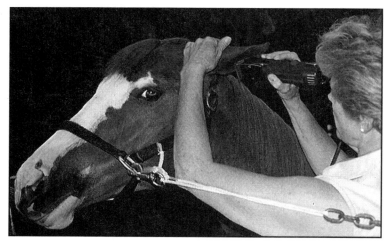

Clip the inside of the ear. Try not to let the hairs fall into the ear canal as an ear infection may result. You can put cotton into the ear prior to clipping.

"deluxe" trim for the shows. In between, just get close enough to make it look neat.

CLIPPING ENHANCES THE FACE

After shaving the bridle path, switch to a number-forty blade and shave the muzzle hairs or whiskers to give the head a neat, chiseled appearance. Trim the long hairs under the jaw and cheeks of the horse, blending upward to the top of the nose and face. Be sure to also clip the small hairs inside the nostrils. If your horse has a blaze, star, strip, or snip, clip the white hairs of the marking and blend the clipped white hairs into the solid hairs of the face. Blend the uncut dark hair into the white clipped hair.

Blending, either on the face or on the legs, is best done by turning the clippers over and holding them upside-down as you blend the solid-colored hairs into the white hairs. Hold the clippers lightly in your hand. Gripping them tightly makes the clippers dig into the hair and cut more than is necessary.

Finally, cut the eye whiskers, *not the lashes,* to finish the picture. Cover the horse's eye with your free hand to protect it in case your horse moves, and clip the long whiskers above the eye. Close the horse's eye to clip the lower whiskers.

Still using the number-forty blade, shave out the inside of the ears. Be careful not to let the hair fall into the ear canal or it could cause an infection. Block the ear canal with a finger or piece of cotton. Gently bend the ear back so that you can reach the hairs inside the ears and clip those out. (Being too rough will cause your horse to resist his next clipping.) Then, in one smooth pass,

to the end of the bridle path, you might cut a few more hairs each time, making your bridle path longer, until it is past the accepted length. Your bridle path will become an eighth-inch longer than the original measurement, then a quarter inch longer, then a half inch, and so on. By the end of the show season, your bridle path could end up being an inch or more longer than where you started. Save the

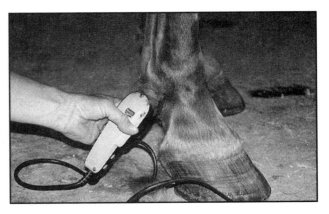

Clip up the leg to remove the long hair on the fetlocks.

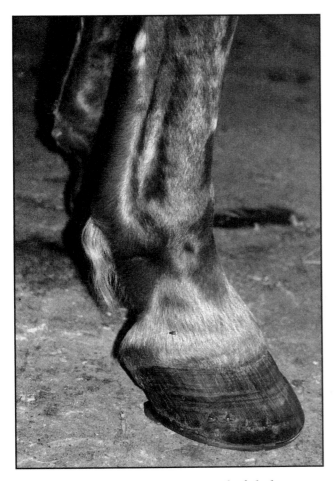

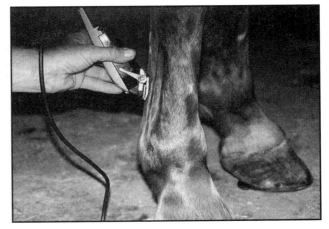

You must remove the long feathers on the fetlock.

And clip down to feather the edges together.

run the clippers from the top of the ear to the bottom, taking off the long hairs on the edge of the ear in one pass. This leaves the ear clipped neatly. Square off the tip of the ear by clipping straight across the top of it. This is an optical illusion that makes ears look shorter. Clip or neaten any hair near the base of the ears and the area between the ear and the bridle path. Gently lay the forelock to one side and clip any short hairs on each side. The forelock should be somewhat thin and should lie flat. Thinning the mane is discussed in Chapter 14.

After the head is clipped, move to the legs. Wash them first, because dirty hair will dull your clipper blades. When they have dried, clip the long fetlock hairs, and feather and blend the hair all the way up to the knee or hock. If your horse has a white sock or stocking, you should "boot" the legs for a registered or breed show. This means to shave all the white hair off the leg to the knee or hock, then blend the clipped area into the solid-colored area above. On a solid-colored leg, just trim around the coronary band so that no long hairs extend onto the hoof.

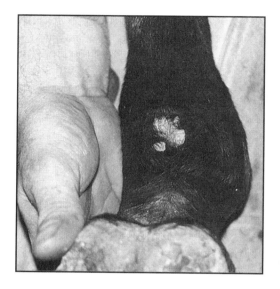

This is an ergot. Clip around these.

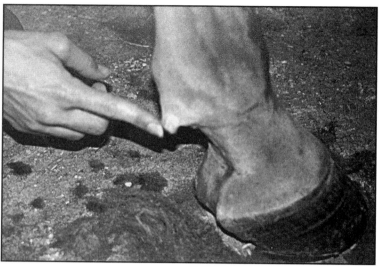

You can ask your farrier to trim the ergots to skin level.

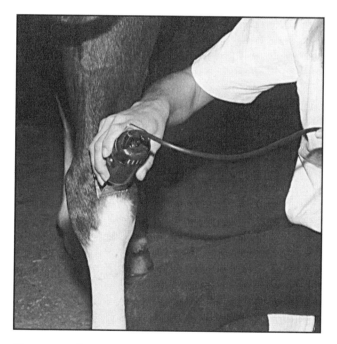

Run your clippers downward to blend the colored hair into the clipped white hair.

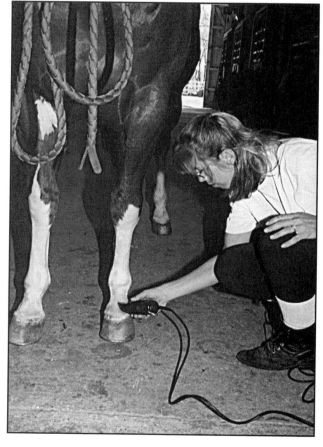

On white legs, clip the white hair to boot the leg.

This gives a neat, trim appearance.

After you clip the legs, trim or clip the ergots back to skin level, or ask your farrier to trim them. Ergots are the little protrusions that stick out behind the fetlock. Not all horses have these, so don't be alarmed if you can't find them. The chestnuts, found higher up the legs, also need to be taken to skin level. This can be done more easily after a bath. They will peel more readily after being soaked in water. You can also cover them with oil and let the oil soften them. Clip any hairs that may be sticking up after removing the ergots and chestnuts. Take one last look for any hairs that you might have missed and touch up as needed.

REVIEW

Buy the best clippers that you can afford. If you take good care of them, they will last you a long time. Be sure to keep your blades sharp and the clippers well oiled. Don't drop them or the case may crack. Be sure that the cord doesn't fray and short out the entire unit or shock your horse at an inopportune moment. Cheap clippers not only don't last as long, they don't cut as well. Good clippers are a worthwhile investment if you care for them well.

Take the time to teach your horse not to be afraid of clippers by using the five-step program outlined earlier. The time spent now will pay dividends down the road. Once a horse learns to accept being clipped, you can buckle the halter around his neck, freeing you from having to work around the halter pieces, and your horse will stand and let you clip him with ease.

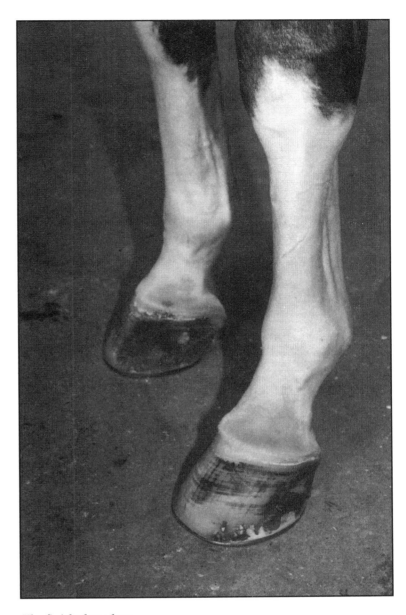

The finished product.

"Studly"—before grooming

. . .and after.

CHAPTER THIRTEEN

GROOMING TO WIN

A GOOD HAIR COAT, as we stated previously, starts on the inside with a proper feeding and worming program and is finished on the outside with a good grooming program. Grooming your horse daily after his workout while his skin is still warm helps bring the natural skin oils to the surface and creates that winning look with lots of shine and sparkle. Grooming should start with a rubber curry and end with a soft-rub rag, with a lot of muscle in between.

Although you should groom a horse before working him to prevent saddle sores, most of your effort should be concentrated after the workout when he has cooled down somewhat. In the early stages of conditioning a horse will sweat easily, making the grooming procedure more difficult. He is wet from sweat, so you must cool him down and then groom. He does not need to be ice cold—that defeats the purpose—but his hair needs to be dry. Do not let sweat dry on his skin because he will become itchy and may rub his tail or other parts of his hair coat. In the summer, of course, you can hose off the sweat with a quick

Preparation for showmanship begins long before that first showmanship class.

Countless hours of grooming time went into these exhibitor's horses prior to showing.

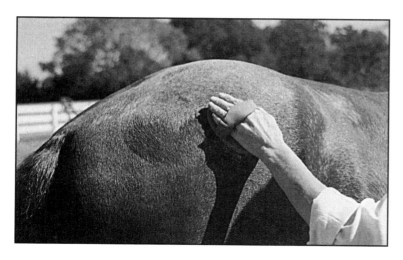

A rubber curry is used in a circular motion to loosen dead hair and dirt, and it helps to bring the oils of the hair to the top. If you do nothing else, curry your horse every day.

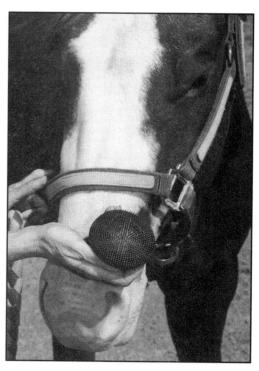

A soft rubber curry is used for the face.

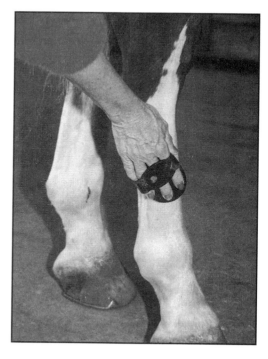

Be sure to curry and clean the legs. Many horses get a fungus on their hind legs from lack of grooming.

rinse and groom him when he is dry. In the cooler months, when hosing is not an option, groom your horse after he dries to avoid having him rub. A well-conditioned horse will not sweat that much and you can groom him right after you have finished working him. In the initial stages of conditioning, if your horse sweats a lot you can work him lightly—just enough to get his skin warm—before grooming him, and then work him harder later in the day. You'll need to find a schedule that works for you and stick to it. Grooming before a workout is acceptable and is certainly better than no grooming.

Your horse should stand either in cross ties or straight tied as he is being groomed. This teaches him that you are in control of his movements and it teaches him patience. Many of my horses get tied for an hour a day, either before or after they are worked. Tying a horse after he is worked teaches him not to rush back to the barn. It is not much fun standing tied to a ring in the wall, and a horse soon learns that rushing back to the barn will only result in having to stand tied for a longer period of time. Another reason to make a horse stand tied for an hour a day is because when you are at a show, he may have to stand tied for a long periods. Unless he-learns to stand patiently, you will be "attached" to your horse for the duration of the show.

I prefer to use the Grooma Groomer®, but a rubber curry works as well. (Use a rubber, not metal, curry—the metal is too harsh on the coat and can break the hair). Use a circular motion to loosen dried hair and dead skin. Really put some muscle into it, unless your horse shows you by his actions that you are using too much pressure and hurting him. Use the curry lightly on the horse's flanks where most horses are quite sensitive, and very lightly on his face. A horse's face and lower legs are made of bones, tendons, and ligaments covered only with skin and no muscle; therefore, your grooming pressure in these areas must be lighter. Groom your horse's face, because his facial hair will shed and must be removed. The same thing applies to his lower legs. Be sure to curry the horse's cannon bones.

Some horses are prone to getting a fungus on the lower legs (most often the back legs) and daily grooming of these areas may easily prevent it from developing. At the least, while grooming you will notice a fungus in the first stages, allowing you to treat it sooner. There are many antifungal shampoos on the market; the best that I've found was purchased from my veterinarian. It was well worth the cost (twenty dollars a bottle), because after one or two applications the fungus cleared up.

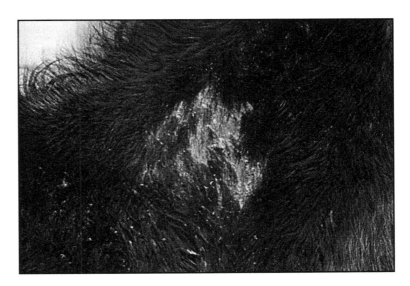

Treat fungus at the first sign of it. This is an extreme case on a horse's neck, left untreated.

If a horse has been pastured for the winter and has a long winter coat, you can use a shedding blade until you see signs of new hair coming in. Then switch to a rubber curry. Even if you use a shedding blade, *use a rubber curry afterward*. It is like a good massage to a horse and will help to stimulate the natural oils in his coat

After currying a horse—and that is where most of your muscle power will be aimed—use a stiff dandy brush to flick the dirt up and away from the hair. Use *short* strokes that lift the loose hair and dirt upward at the end of each stroke. Do this over the horse's entire body, using less pressure on the legs and face, as mentioned earlier. This readies the coat for the final brushing with a softer finishing brush. Go over the horse's entire body with the soft brush, using long strokes, and follow that by rubbing with a soft rub-rag or terry towel.

This entire procedure should take, at a bare minimum, ten minutes. Twenty to thirty minutes is better. Skimping on grooming time

Use short strokes with a stiff dandy brush and...

...flick the dust and dirt up, away from the horse.

Follow the dandy brush with a softer finishing brush.

will show later in the ring when the horses that you're competing against dazzle a judge with their brilliance while your horse lacks the superior hair coat so necessary to win at the larger shows. You *cannot* skimp on grooming time. An added benefit is that, since horses enjoy being groomed, it helps you to build a closer relationship with your horse.

Besides grooming the horse's coat, you must pay attention to his hooves. Good farriers are hard to find—take good care of the relationship when you find the right one. Ask him about the quality and condition of your horse's hooves and how to properly condition them. Pick out and clean your horse's feet *daily*, whether or not you apply hoof dressing. In some areas of the country, thrush seems to be more prevalent. Daily cleaning should help to alleviate any problems with thrush.

After you have groomed your horse and cleaned out his feet, direct your attention to his mane and tail. I use an inexpensive conditioner mixed five to one with water. I apply it after every bath or rinse in the summer, and as often as I can in the winter, weather permitting. Do not rinse it out; rub it in. Make sure that the entire tail is covered with the conditioner, and massage the hair at the horse's tailbone. Never comb a horse's tail when it is wet, as the tail hairs will break. Apply the conditioner and leave the tail alone. The next day, when you groom the horse before working, run a rubber-toothed brush (never a comb) through the tail. A horse's tail takes a very long time to grow, so the fewer hairs you pull out, the less time you will have to wait for them to grow back.

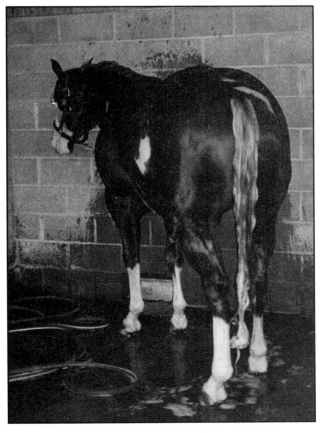

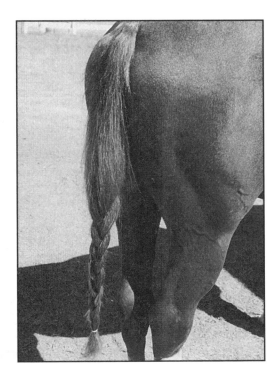

After bathing and rinsing, condition the tail and then braid it to keep it tangle-free...

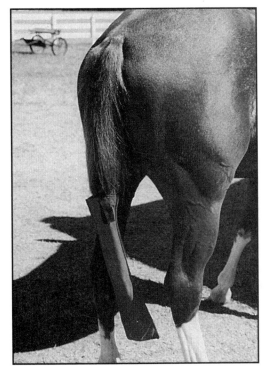

and put it in a tail bag...

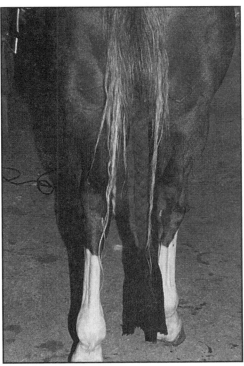

...or braid it into this type of tail bag.

In the Quarter Horse Association, fake tails are currently allowed, but they are expensive and care must be taken with them. If you can keep your horse's natural tail long, silky and shiny, you will save time, effort, and money. If your horse has no tail, a fake tail will add to his overall appearance but is not absolutely required in showmanship and certainly not at the lower levels. If you do choose to buy one, match the colors well and ask the salesperson for help in putting it on correctly.

Your western horse's mane should be kept to a length of about three inches if you are showing a Quarter Horse or Paint. Other breed associations have different rules, so read your rule book or go to a few shows and see what the current style is for the breed of your choice. Quarter Horses and Paints should have their mane pulled, allowing the mane to lie flat on the horse's neck and not be thick and bushy (see Chapter 14). Horses can get crabby about having their mane pulled, and sometimes a horse will only let you do so much on a given day. Rather than getting into a fight, do a little over a few days until finally the mane is even enough so that you can band it easily.

A horse that is showing at a Quarter Horse or Paint show should have his bridle path clipped Hold the ear back against his neck and clip even with the tip of his ears. Other associations have different rules.

Your horse can be blanketed in the fall, winter, and spring. You can fool your horse into thinking that it is always summer by adding the warmth from a blanket and a light in his stall for eighteen hours a day. Care must be taken that the horse

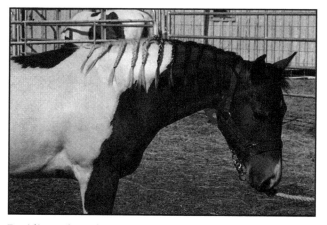

Braiding a horse's mane when he is a yearling will help to train it to lie over on one side of the neck.

A Slinky is the most helpful grooming aid to teach a horse's mane to lie over flat.

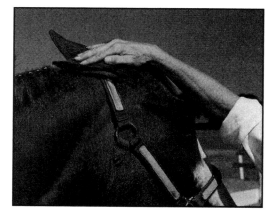

The bridle path should be clipped to the length of the horse's ear.

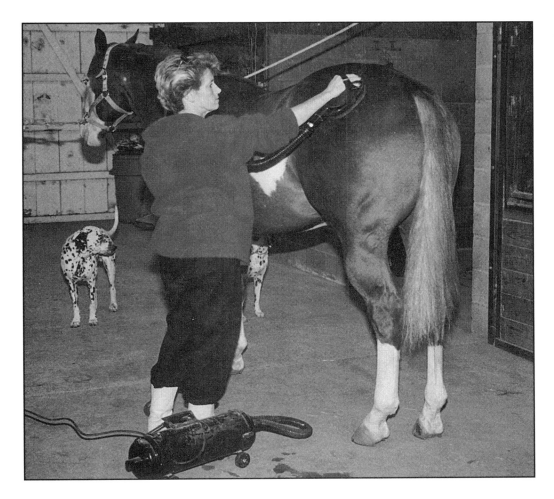

A horse vacuum is a handy tool that can be used year-round.

does not become too hot under the blanket and sweat. If he does, he'll rub and might ruin his hair coat, mane, or tail. This means that he might need one, two, or even three blankets overnight, and you might need to change to a sheet during the day. A hood will help to keep his body heat from escaping, and a Slinky or similar type of hood will make his mane lie smoothly on his neck.

The hardest part about blanketing a horse through the winter is that you must be available to change the weight or amount of blankets as the day warms. Once you start using a blanket, you cannot turn the horse out in cold weather with no hair to protect him from the cold. Some nights I go back to the barn at ten

p.m. to blanket horses.

An alternative to blanketing is to let your horse grow hair and put him under lights ninety days before you need to have him slick and show-ready. However, a good blanketing system will save you from the long, shaggy hair coat when spring rolls around. You almost have to blanket if you want to enter early shows. And you must be prepared to start early in the fall, at least with your lighting system, to fool the horse's system into thinking that it is summer year-round.

A good grooming system takes time, effort, and muscle. But, the results are worth the slick, shiny hair coat that will leave your competitors drooling with envy.

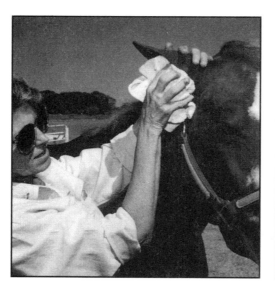 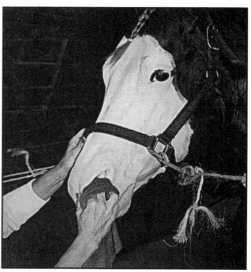

Teach your horse to accept having his ears...   *...and his nose cleaned.*

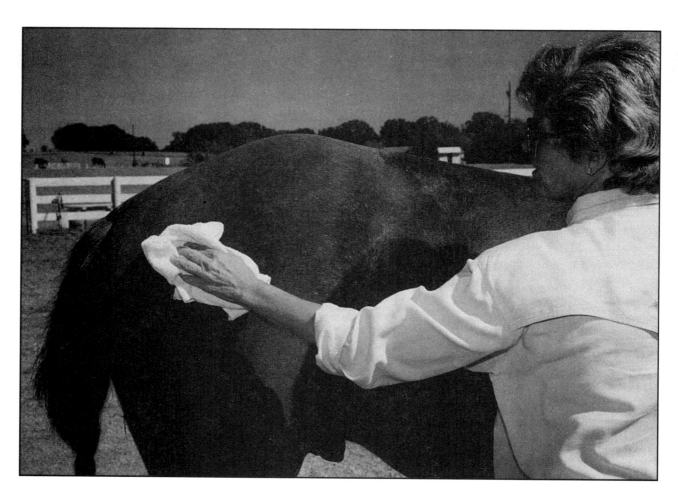

Finish the job by rubbing the horse's coat all over with a soft, clean towel.

CHAPTER FOURTEEN

BANDING THE MANE

BANDING A HORSE'S MANE is simply taking small sections of mane and using a small elastic—the same one used to contain braids on an English horse—to section a mane into little segments so that it lies neatly down the horse's neck. While banding is not absolutely required, it has become the accepted manner in which to show your horse, especially at the higher levels. Banding presents a finished, professional picture. A correctly banded mane says to the judge that you have done your homework and spent the extra time that banding takes to show your horse to his best potential. Obviously, banding a horse's mane doesn't guarantee you a ribbon, but the banded horse looks neater and that little extra effort may be just enough to sway the judge in your favor.

When you band a horse, a judge assumes that you have previously spent hours pulling the mane to the desired thickness and length and practicing so that your bands come out neatly, with each band the same size as the last one. The bands should lie neatly along the horse's neck and not stick up in the air.

Putting your horse in a mane tamer or Slinky overnight will help to keep his mane neatly on one side of his neck. This too, takes that little extra effort that helps present a polished, professional picture. You can, of course, pay someone to band your horse or beg a friend to do it, but the impression the judge has is still the same—that you are willing to put in the time to make your horse look his absolute best.

A correctly banded mane has approximately forty bands down the length of a horse's neck. A long-necked horse might have a few more and a short-necked horse a few less, but forty is an average number that will help you get the desired look. Experiment a little. If too many bands make your horse's neck look too long, use fewer bands, and vice versa.

BAND ON THE RIGHT SIDE

Assuming that your horse has a good neck that you want to show

107

off, train his mane to lie on the right side of his neck. In this way, the judge's first impression of your horse (on the left side, because you enter the arena and travel counterclockwise) is of a sleek, trim neck. It is not essential that your horse's mane lie on the right side, but it is preferable if your horse has a nice, clean neck. If you want to hide your horse's neck, do the opposite and band on the left side.

EMPHASIZE GOOD POINTS

Your job is to show off your horse's good points and minimize his faults. Remember that this class was started as a way to teach handlers to show halter horses. While showmanship is judged on the handler, the handler is being judged on *his ability to show a halter horse,* and a halter class is judged on the *horse.* Therefore, a judge is ultimately looking for a handler to whom he could turn over his best horse and win the World show. The better you can make your horse look, the better handler you are—in a judge's mind. A properly banded horse, presented the right way, again conveys to the judge that you have done your homework and understand the intricacies of showing at halter.

PULL THE MANE

If your horse's mane is too thick or too long to band neatly, you will first have to pull it to shorten it. Pulling a mane is exactly what it says—pulling some

See how pulling and shortening enhances this horse's already pretty neck.

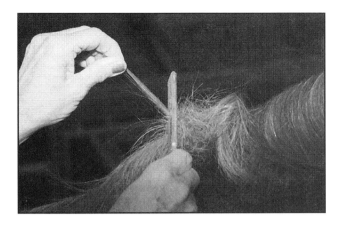

1) *To pull a horse's mane, grasp a small section of hair and then tease most of it back with a comb, leaving a few hairs in your fingers.*

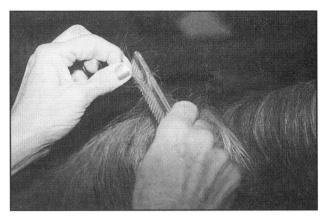

2) *Wrap those remaining hairs around the comb...*

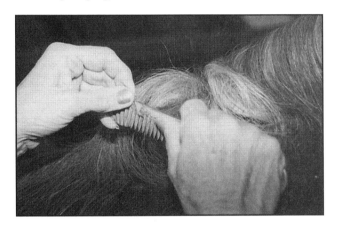

3) *and yank them out quickly.*

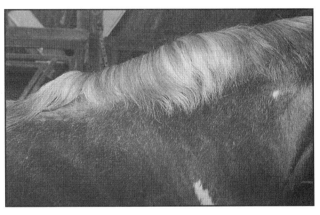

4) *Notice the thinned and shortened section achieved by pulling.*

of the hairs to thin the mane. As you thin, you'll probably shorten at the same time. If the mane is still too long after pulling, or if your horse has a thin mane that is just too long and does not need to be pulled first, use thinning shears or a razor knife to shorten the mane. Thinning shears and razor knives do not thin a mane; they merely shorten one that is already the desired thickness. Either tool will avoid the blunt-cut look that you get by using ordinary scissors.

The mane should be kept about three inches in length. If you pull or shorten at the beginning of the show season, you will most likely have to shorten it again later. I find it easier to pull and shorten a longer mane. *Do not use scissors to get a shorter length first.* Leave the mane long, pull as much as you need to get the desired thinness, then take the thinning shears, if needed, to shorten it more.

To pull a mane, take a section of hair in your hand and put the comb above those hairs. Push most of the hairs back by "teasing" them upward. This should leave you with just a few hairs in your hand. Wrap those hairs once around your comb, give a quick, sharp tug and pull the hairs out at the roots. Work your way up the mane.

Next, *after the mane is pulled and thinned to the correct thickness,* make a straight line up the horse's neck with the thinning scissors. Now half or more of the mane is already at the correct length, and you have a straight line left by the thinning shears to follow. Finishing the job is easy—use a razor knife to cut the small pieces that the thinning shears missed. Grab small sections of hair with the razor knife and cut them. If one or two long hairs remain, you can use regular scissors to clean them up—just don't blunt-cut the mane.

PREPARATION AND PRACTICE BANDING

The best thing about a horse's mane—as long as you don't wait until the day before a show to begin to practice—is that it *will* grow back. Practice pulling and shortening a few times until you master the technique, or make your first attempts on a broodmare or a horse that is not immediately headed for the show ring. The more you practice, the better you'll become. It is always helpful to find a friend who can give you some pointers. Don't be afraid to ask for help.

If you are banding your horse's mane for practice—not the night before a show—don't wash the mane first. A dirty mane is easier to band. *Do not condition your horse's mane or use glycerine-based products on it before you band!* The hairs will slip right out of your hands.

When you are ready to begin banding, first gather your supplies.

You'll need a mane comb and brush. I use a hair brush with rubber teeth that will not damage the hairs. A comb—even a plastic one—is too harsh to use on a horse's mane or tail. I never use a mane comb except to section the mane. You will need a supply of elastics or braiding bands, either white or in a color to match your horse's mane. Use bands made for braiding an English horse's mane. They are available in tack stores or through equine catalogues.

The easiest way to be sure the sections of mane are of uniform size is to use a plastic braiding comb. Rather than use the three sections, as you would if you were braiding, take just one section and band that. A large hair clip, found at any health and beauty-aid department, will hold the balance of the horse's mane out of the way as you work. Finally, you'll need a towel and a small pail of water, or a spray bottle filled with water, so you can keep the hair damp. A damp mane is easier to handle. Either place the towel over the horse's mane to wet it, or spritz the mane with the spray bottle. As you work your way down the horse's neck, keep repeating the process as needed to keep the hair damp.

THE BANDING PROCEDURE

If the mane lies on the right side of the horse's neck, I start at the bottom and work my way up because I am left-handed. If I have the mane on the left side of the neck, perhaps to hide a thick neck or some other problem that I don't want the judge to see, I start at the top and work down to the withers. If you are right-handed, reverse the process. (Mane on the right—start

1) To band, take a section of hair the width of which is no bigger than your smallest finger. Clip the balance of the hair back out of your way.

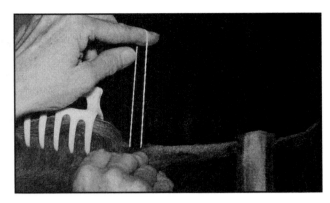

2) Place the hair through the elastic.

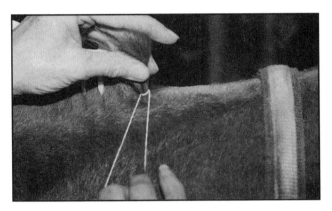

3) Twist the elastic and pull down.

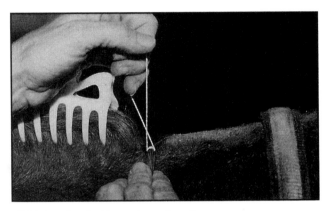

4) Twist the elastic again and pull up.

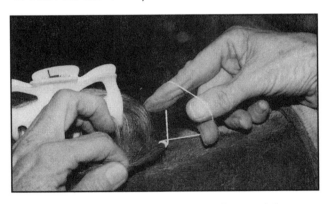

5) Continue to twist the elastic and pull up and down.

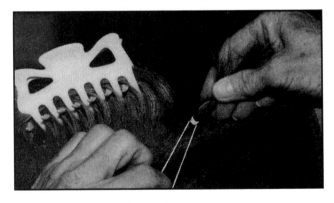

6) Be sure that your last twist ends down.

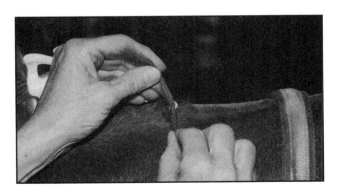

7) Pull a few hairs from the underside to make the bands lay flat.

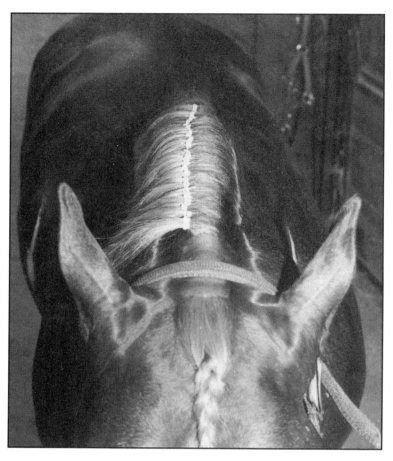

Your end result should have all bands lying flat and evenly spaced down the horse's neck.

resting on the horse's back. Some people put them in their mouth to hold them, but if you do this, be sure not to swallow or you might choke.

The simplest way to band quickly is to double the elastic before you begin to band a section of mane. In this way, you wrap once around the section of mane from the top side down, ending with the long section of the elastic at the under part of the mane. Your next twist and wrap brings you to the top of the horse's mane again, and the final twist and wrap brings your elastic back down underneath, or to the bottom of, the horse's mane. Whether you choose to double your elastic or you prefer to use it single and then wrap it five or six times, your last twist and wrap *should end up at the underside, or bottom, of the horse's mane.* This helps to make the mane lie flat on the horse's neck.

Use the braiding comb again to get your next section of hair, and repeat the entire process. Continue up (or down) the horse's neck until you have completed the entire mane. If the bands are sticking up in the air a little, reach underneath and take just a few hairs from that part closest to the underside of the neck and pull them downward, close to the horse's neck. This will help the sections of mane lie flatter on the horse's neck and give a neater appearance. Try to keep all of your elastics side by side, neatly lined up in a row. If one or two are out of line, you may need to undo them and repeat the process. The more times that you practice banding, the neater your bands will become and the sooner you will finish.

Unless you are banding your horse's mane to help train it to lie all

at the top. Mane on the left—start at the bottom.) Use your braiding comb to make three sections of mane. Take the farthest *single* section of mane, depending on which direction is easier for you to start with, and use the hair clip to hold the balance of the horse's mane out of the way. (Although the braiding comb will make three sections of mane, you can only band one at a time. Take the farthest section and let the other two go, held to the side by your hair clamp.)

To keep your tools handy, either stick the braiding comb in your pocket or put it on your horse's back. I keep a supply of elastics either around one of my fingers or on one side or the other, take the bands out when you are done practicing or showing. If, however, you want to train a mane to lie on one side of a horse's neck, you can leave the bands in for a couple of days. Just be aware that your horse might rub and, in so doing, pull out a section or more of his mane. Leaving a Slinky or mane tamer on overnight is perhaps a safer way to train a horse's mane to stay on the correct side.

CONDITION YOUR HORSE'S MANE AND TAIL

Wash and condition your horse's mane every couple of days to encourage it to lie to one side. Make sure that all soap is rinsed out or it will itch and make your horse rub, sometimes taking out complete sections of the mane. In addition to, or perhaps in place of, a Slinky (if you do not have one or if it is too hot to use one) a neck sweat will help train the mane to lie to one side. After working the horse with the neck sweat on, rinse the sweat off his neck so that he doesn't want to rub because of dried sweat. Then place the mane on the correct side and brush it down, using cold water to help keep it flat.

I use a conditioner, mixed five to one with water. Whether I've washed the horse's mane and tail or not, I apply this conditioner every day, except the day before a show, unless it is extremely cold. The conditioner keeps the mane and tail soft and tangle-free and gives that soft, well-cared-for look. This conditioner also seems to help a tail grow rather quickly.

If your horse has a white tail, keep it as clean as possible. That may mean rinsing or even washing it daily. I never rinse conditioner out of a tail unless it is the day before a show. It keeps the tail soft and helps it to grow. The day before a show, I use a mane- and tail-whitening product, available through any of the equine catalogues or at your favorite tack store. With most of these whitening products, you must first wash the mane and tail and rinse them well. Mix the whitening agent according to the directions on the label, and apply. Let it sit for five minutes (or however long the directions say) then rinse thoroughly again. Apply conditioner to the tail (unless you plan to braid it). Do not apply conditioner to the mane or you will not be able to band it without the hairs sliding right out of your fingers. Wait for the tail to dry.

I often braid the whole length of a horse's tail the night before a show. Braiding helps to give a tail added thickness. When you unbraid it just before your class, some of the waves remain, giving the tail a fuller look. I almost always wrap the tail the night before a show. Wrapping keeps the hairs on top of the tailbone flat and shows off a horse's hindquarters. If a horse has a "bad" hind end, or perhaps something that I want to hide, such as a scar, then I do not wrap the tail, preferring instead to hide the blemish.

When wrapping, make a wrap or two around the tail, then flip a few tail hairs *up* so that you can wrap around them. With the next wrap, fold any hairs *down* that were left showing. Then repeat the entire procedure a few wraps further down the tail. These little hairs will hold the tail wrap in place, and in the morning, a quick brushing with cold water will make those few hairs that you folded up lie flat again.

FINISH THE MANE AND TAIL BEFORE A SHOW

Before you band for a show, be sure that your horse's mane is clean first. Wash it, *but do not condition it.* On most horses, I band the night before the show and cover the horse's neck with a Slinky or mane tamer. This helps to hold the mane down flat and it keeps the horse's neck from getting dirty. If you have previously noticed your horse rubbing his mane when banded, wait until the day of the show to do your banding.

I use a human hair spray called Freeze® just before class to keep the mane lying flat and not flying in the wind if there is a breeze. Placing a clean saddle pad over the entire length of the horse's neck directly after applying the hair spray also helps to hold the hair down. Carefully spray the forelock, too, but be sure that you don't get the chemical in the horse's eyes. Run your hand down the forelock until it lies flat. Do the same to the tail. Spray the top of the tail heaviest and run your hands down the tailbone to give a neater look to the tail, keeping the wispy hairs near the top of the tail flat against the tailbone. Apply hair spray very lightly to the balance of the tail. A light misting of Grand Champion® or Show Sheen®, a quick, last-minute rub with the grooming towel, and a touch-up of hoof black, if necessary, should finish the picture. You're ready to enter the arena.

CHAPTER FIFTEEN

CHOOSING THE RIGHT TACK

GOOD, CLEAN, well-fitting tack (halter and lead line) is expected of all showmanship exhibitors. The type or style of halter that you use and how you adjust the fit can add to or detract from your horse's face. A halter should hug your horse's face, not hang loosely below it. A small, attractive-headed mare can be enhanced by a feminine type of halter, while the same halter will look out of place on a big, stoutly built gelding. A large, heavy horse needs a halter that shows off his head but is suitable for his size. On the same note, a young horse will "swim" in a halter made for an adult. Halters come in weanling, yearling, cob, and horse sizes, to name a few. Select a halter that fits your horse snugly and that also enhances his face.

Most showmanship halters are made of leather with silver accents. For a local or 4-H show, a plain leather halter will suffice, but when you progress to the bigger shows, a nice halter trimmed with silver is almost a requirement. The size and type of silver that you choose can add to or detract from your horse's face.

Your halter must be in style with those of the other competitors in your show. If you are planning to buy a halter, it is wise to attend a few shows at the level in which you plan to participate and observe the current styles. For example, if you are planning to enter a 4-H competition, a halter with less silver might suffice. However, at open and breed shows, your horse will look out of place with a plain halter. It is at this level and above that you will see the leather halters with silver accents, although many 4-H exhibitors also use them. Some judges at the open-level shows might not penalize you for a well-fitting, very clean, plain leather halter, but in general, if you are planning to compete seriously in a showmanship class, use a well-fitting, silver-trimmed one.

Such a halter is an expensive investment. If you are not yet sure that showmanship is something you want to do long-term, start with a used silver halter. Once you have made the decision to compete seriously in this class, purchase a good silver-accented halter strictly for showmanship or halter classes. Use it when

Watching the judge, waiting for the cue to begin. This exhibor's professional attitude, together with a neatly groomed and clipped horse, creates that winning look. You can see how, even from a distance, the silver on this halter sets off the horse's head.

An Arabian show halter is much more refined.

you show and put it away safely the rest of the time. This is not the halter you use to tie your horse to the trailer. The silver will lose its shape if it is bent incorrectly, and some of the fine silver lacework may snap off, leaving you no choice but to either find a jeweler who can repair the silver or buy a new halter. When you leave the ring, take your good halter off your horse, immediately and replace it with your everyday one. If you do this, your initial purchase can last for many years.

A CORRECTLY FITTING HALTER

The noseband of your horse's halter should fit comfortably yet somewhat snugly around his nose. When you run your hand down the front of the horse's face, you will feel where the bone ends and the cartilage begins. Adjust the noseband of the halter so it lies right above that point. Another good rule of thumb is that the noseband should lie about an inch below the bottom of the horse's cheekbone. The noseband should not droop—that detracts from your horse's face. The better (and more expensive) leather halters will have an adjustable noseband so that you can fit the halter correctly. If there are buckles on either side of the halter, adjust them both, rather than adjusting only one side. You want the adjustment to be symmetrical.

The crown piece of the halter should lie right behind the horse's ears. The throat latch should fall neatly at the base of the horse's cheekbone, not hang loosely in front of it. If there is an adjustment on either side of the crown piece, adjust both sides for a symmetrical appearance. Your halter should fit comfortably on the horse, yet look somewhat like a snug-fitting glove.

With a correct length chain, just snap to the ring as shown. Run the chain under his chin and up the side of the halter as shown on the left.

The chain can be shortened as shown on the right.

A LEAD LINE

A leather lead line with a chain is the proper equipment for showmanship. Run the chain of the lead line through the left side halter ring, under the jaw, and through the ring on the opposite side. Then run it up to the top ring of the halter on the right side. The chain should extend about four inches out from the left halter ring, allowing you to hold the lead line shank, *not the chain,* and still easily maintain control of your horse. Holding the *chain* of the lead shank is a major fault, and you will be severely penalized for it. In fact, a judge will penalize you for even touching the chain. If your chain is too long, take it to a saddle shop and have it shortened. In a last-minute emergency, double the chain back through the top ring of the cheek piece of your halter and snap it to itself to shorten it. However, plan to have it shortened at the first possible chance.

You don't need to practice at home with your show halter, but be sure that it fits before you leave for your first show. You may need to make minor adjustments. You might need to punch more holes or the length of the chain may need to be adjusted, and the minutes before your class are not the time to find this out.

When you are schooling at home, you can use any nylon or leather halter with a lead line and chain. You must teach your horse at home to obey your commands with the chain under his chin. The "pull" on the halter is different with a chain under his nose as compared to the pull from a lead line attached to the ring of his halter. Use the chain under his chin to clue the horse that you are now working on showmanship. He is not being led to the turnout area—he will be working. Some horses, when first faced with the pull of a chain under their nose, will rear or pull back, so don't wait until the day of the show to suddenly put the chain under your horse's nose and expect him to behave.

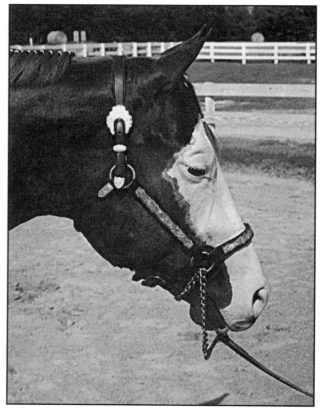

While the halter now fits correctly, the chain is incorrectly looped under the jaw.

This is all wrong. It shows lack of attention to detail. Not only will you lose points for ill-fitting tack, it tells the judge you have not done your homework. You have not learned how a halter should fit and/or you do not care to take the time to fit it correctly to the horse. In either case, the judge will not consider you a serious contender. By shortening the crown piece, the throat latch would move up to the correct position and fit snugly behind the jowl of the horse. The chain should run through the ring and up the side as illustrated earlier. The keepers of the noseband have not been used and this makes it look sloppy. Pay attention to detail!

Again the chain is incorrect. The halter is too large for this yearling and cannot be adjusted to fit properly. You must buy a halter that fits your horse. (Just a Spot Away owned by Joanne Chiron, Harwinton, Connecticut.)

A correctly fitted halter. The noseband should lie halfway between eye and nose and fit snugly. The throat latch is snug and neat, and all keepers are in place.

Well-fitting tack enhances this stallion's already attractive head. Photo by Evelyn McKinney.

Remember, *whenever you use a chain* under a horse's nose, you must always use the pull-and-release. A steady pull on a chain run under the jaw may cause the horse to rear and possibly flip over backward. This is why it is mandatory to practice at home with the chain under the chin. Don't leave anything to chance. Practice the same way you will present the horse at a show—never surprise your horse at a show by trying something new.

After a show, take your halter and lead line home and clean and oil them if necessary. There are special bags made for holding halters and bridles. Put your tack in a safe place. Keep your leather clean and oiled. Use silver polish or a silver-polishing cloth on the silver to keep it sparkling clean. Do this routinely after every show and it will always be ready for your next showmanship class.

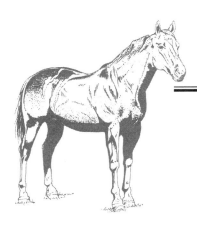

SHOWING THE ENGLISH HORSE

SHOWING AN ENGLISH HORSE in showmanship classes is similar to showing a western horse, with just a few exceptions. English horses are shown in hand with a bridle, rather than with a halter as western horses are shown. An "O" or "D" ring snaffle, is one of the most common bits in which to show. In areas of the country where the western horse dominates, you will also see a Kimberwick. (Many western horses use a curb bit, and the Kimberwick has a similar mouthpiece, making the switch from a curb to a Kimberwick an easy one.)

CHECK YOUR BREED ASSOCIATION RULES

The horse himself should be set up square or stretched, according to his breed association rules. Quarter Horses, Paints, and most other stock breeds are set up with all four legs placed squarely underneath them. Morgans, Arabians, and most gaited horses are stretched, meaning that the front legs are forward rather than squarely underneath the body. Always check with your breed association for the rules that apply to your breed.

For the breeds that are shown stretched, set the back feet as stated

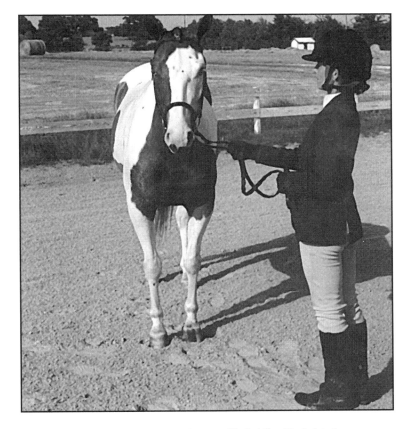

Showing the English horse with a snaffle bridle. Had this been an actual show, the horse's hooves would have been blackened.

earlier. Lift the horse's head, but do not pull him forward or ask him to walk forward. Using a dressage-style whip, tap behind the fetlock on his left front leg. As soon as he moves it foward even slightly, stop taping and praise. Let the horse ab-

121

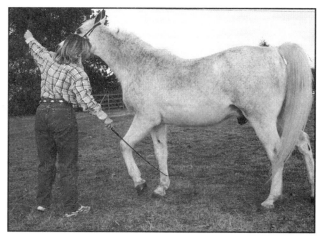

To teach a horse to stretch, lift the lead-line and tap the left front foot forward. Stop tapping and praise as soon as the horse picks the foot up to move it forward.

Then work on the right front foot. Always stop tapping as soon as the horse moves the foot. Reward even the smallest steps forward.

sorb that for a bit, then repeat, asking him to move the right front leg. Lifting his head becomes the cue to stretch, so make sure that you lift his head decisively. Ask for another left, then another right, step with the front until he is set according to your breed standard. Be sure to praise for tiny steps forward iniially. Remember, training takes time.

An English horse's mane and tail are braided. A Quarter Horse or Paint is clipped as outlined previously in this book, but Arabians and gaited horses are clipped a bit differently, with longer bridle paths, so once again, it is necessary to check your rules.

If you don't have the benefit of a trainer or instructor nearby, and you show a horse of a different breed, go to a few larger shows in your area prior to entering your first class. Observe how the horses are braided and clipped. Look at the style of clothes that the top exhibitors are wearing. Remember that the larger the show, the better dressed the exhibitors.

DRESS CONSERVATIVELY

Remember, the English or hunt seat classes are always conservative. Traditional hunt-seat attire is a form-fitting jacket in solid navy or

Arabian handlers use a whip to make the horse tip his ears forward. If you plan to show in an open Arabian show, be sure that your horse is not frightened of a whip.

green. A dark blue base color with small pinstripes is also acceptable. Breeches are mandatory, with tall leather boots for adults. Jodhpurs are acceptable for children. Both require the traditional black hunt cap. Saddle seat is slightly different. A derby (hat) replaces the hunt cap, and a longer jacket replaces the hunt coat.

On hot days, the exhibitors at a local show may show without jackets. But you must *wait for that announcement*. At some local or barn shows, jackets and breeches are not absolutely required, but it is best to check with the show secretary prior to arriving. The *proper* way to show hunt-seat showmanship is while wearing breeches, jackets, boots, gloves, and a hard hat

Women's hair should be neatly contained in a hair net under a hunt cap. Small post or clip-on earrings are suitable. A choker with a

English attire is conservative. Breeches, boots, shirt with matching choker, earrings, hard hat and gloves.

stock pin is mandatory, as are dark-colored gloves.

Boots should be clean and sparkling before you enter the arena. Carry a cloth to the arena gate and wipe any dust, mud, or dirt off your boots before entering.

Check your horse to be sure that he has not snitched a bit of grass along the way and has green froth coming from his mouth when he goes into the ring. Make sure that all keepers on your bridle have the leather ends tucked neatly in and that no straps are left hanging.

ATTEND LARGER SHOWS

Attend a few bigger shows, if only to prepare yourself for when you make it to those same bigger shows. Watch the horses that place on top. Ask questions of the com-petitors. Horse people are great; most of them will gladly answer any questions you might have, provided you don't catch them when they are rushing to their next class.

Practice at home *with your horse wearing the bridle that you will show in* until you are absolutely comfortable with your horse and with the equipment, and you know the maneuvers by heart. Then go to a few schooling shows to gain ring experience.

Practice the various maneuvers (which are the same basic exercises we've discussed throughout this book) repeatedly until you can put any of the maneuvers together in a seamless presentation. You'll soon be on your way to gaining those blue ribbons.

When showing in a bridle, keep one finger between the reins and close your hand around them. Hold your hand about four or five inches under the horse's chin, keeping even pressure on both reins. The balance of the reins are held in the left hand. Walk in line with the horse's throat latch.

CHAPTER SEVENTEEN

THE FRENCH BRAID

DOES YOUR HORSE have a long, beautiful, flowing mane that you just can't cut, yet you'd like to show in a hunt-seat showmanship class? Then consider a French braid. Once you try it, you may never go back to those little button braids again. At first glance it may look as if the French braid takes a long time. In reality, it is quick and easy. It takes less than five minutes to braid a mane that hangs below a horse's neck. Add another five minutes to braid his tail, two minutes to braid his forelock, and a few more minutes to be sure he is thoroughly groomed. Add a bit of fly spray and polish his hooves, and you're ready to show.

HOW TO START

To begin the French braid, start at the top of the horse's neck by taking three thin sections of mane—just as if you were going to make a regular braid. If the mane is too fine and slips easily out of your fingers, or the hair flies in all directions, take a sponge and wet the mane, or use a light coating of hairsetting gel first. This will make the hair easier to manage. Never use conditioner or Show Sheen® on the mane right before braiding or the hair will slide not only right out of your hands, but right out of the braid.

Hold the three sections of hair as if you were making a single braid. (Follow the directions accompanying these photos and it will be easier for you to understand.) After starting the first braid with a cross-under of all three sections of hair, begin the French braid by adding another small section of the horse's mane. Use the little finger on your right hand if the horse's mane hangs on the left side of the neck. If it hangs on the right side of the neck, you'll have to use the little finger of your left hand. Grasp a small, new section of hair to add to the braid, separating it with your little finger. That new section of hair goes underneath the braid that you started and joins the next middle section of hair. Make one more cross-under on the braid. Grasp another section of hair and continue to braid. Add a new section of hair every time you make another section of braid.

Continue to work down the mane in this manner until you run out of hair at the base of the horse's neck. At that point, with the three sections of hair still in your hands, finish with a regular braid and braid to the end. Put a small braiding band on the end of the braid to keep it from unraveling.

To finish the French braid, bring the end of your final braid underneath to make a small loop, and put another braiding band on it to keep it in place. The end result looks like a neat plait down your horse's neck with a small loop of braid at the end.

KEEP IT TIGHT AGAINST THE HORSE'S CREST

The secret to a neat French braid is keeping the hairs tight against the horse's neck. Each time you add a section, carefully pull the hairs as tight as you can against the crest of the horse's neck while you carefully braid your way down. When you reach the end of your horse's mane, secure the braid with two elastics as suggested above

and you are done.

It is helpful to put the horse in cross ties if he will stand quietly in them. Also, before starting, put fly spray on the horse so that he will not be tempted to shake his head at an inopportune time and pull the hair out of your hands. If that happens, you usually have to start all over at the top of the neck, because the braid loosens. With practice, it should take you a matter of minutes to complete a French braid.

UNDO THE BRAID

Another advantage of the French braid becomes evident when you are done showing. This braid is easy to undo. Remove the two elastics, then, using your fingers, gently separate the hairs as you work your way up the neck. (Don't use a comb or you'll cause the hair to break.) Use your fingers to remove any tangles, and finish with a soft brush. Be sure to undo the French braid as soon as possible. Never leave it in. If the horse rubs his neck, he'll tear his mane.

A nice mane length to braid.

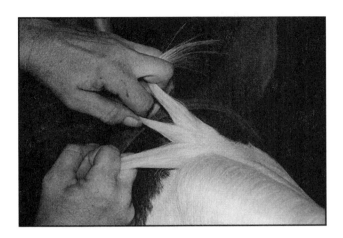

1) Begin the French braid by separating three small sections of mane hair.

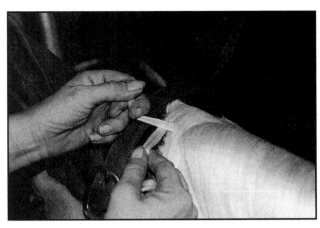

2) Start a braid with one cross under and twist of each section of hair.

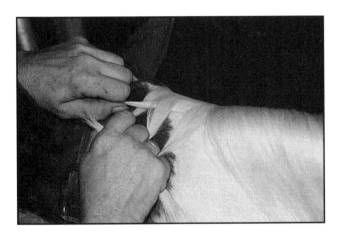

3) Next, with your little finger, pick up a small section of hair from the right—most section of the mane and bring it under...

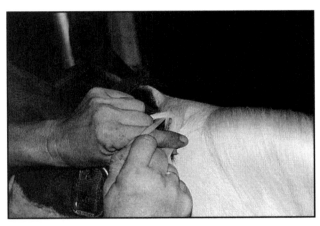

4) so that it adds to, and becomes part of...

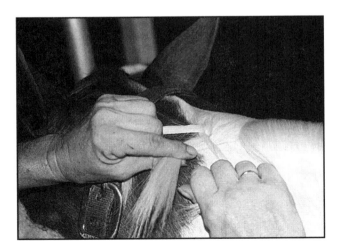

5) the middle section of your braid. It may seem complicated, but practice will make it easier.

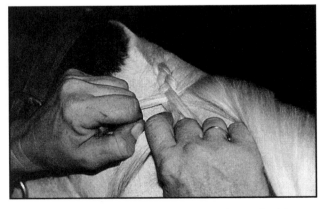

6) Now bring the section at the far left of your braid under so that it becomes the middle section. Don't get confused. Just follow instructions and it should come out right in the end.

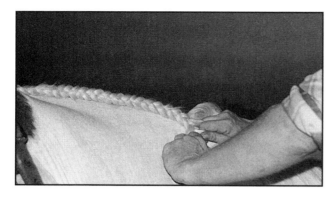

7) As before, pick up another section of hair and bring that section under to add to, and become, the braid's next middle section. Then take the hair on the far left so that it now is the middle section of the braid. Take the right-most section, bring it under to make the braid, and add another section of hair from the right to that middle section. Then continue. Your braid should begin to show proper appearance.

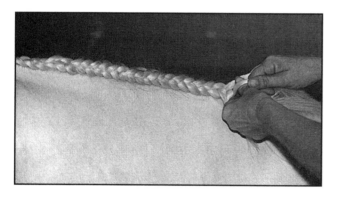

8) Each time moves are made, you must add a section of the remaining hair. Separate it with your little finger and bring it underneath, adding it to the middle section of your braid.

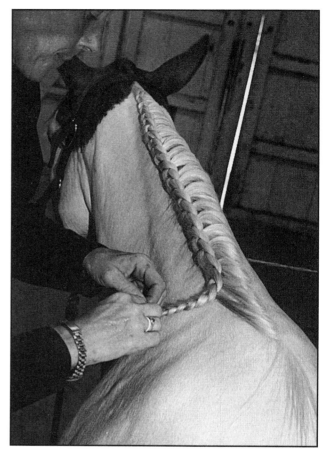

9) With the mane French braided to the end, finish off with a regular braid. Braid to the end of the hairs and wrap with an elastic band.

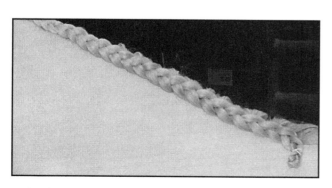

10) Take that braid, loop it underneath, and put another elastic on the end. Your horse's mane is now French braided.

CHAPTER EIGHTEEN

MANE AND BUTTON BRAIDS

BRAIDING AN ENGLISH HORSE with conventional braids can be a time-consuming chore, but with practice, you will increase your speed and also the quality of your braiding job. Practice braiding at least a few braids every day for a couple of weeks or even a month before your first show. When your show date arrives, braid the night before your show if at all possible (unless, of course, you know that the horse will rub and try to pull the braids out).

Many smaller open shows do not require braiding. However, when you move up to a higher level, you'll find most, if not all, English or hunter-type horses braided. For that reason, it is wise to practice and to keep your skills sharp. Braiding is similar to banding—it just takes longer and requires a little more skill.

Before you can think about braiding, your horse's mane must be pulled and shortened (see Chapter 14.) If you plan to braid instead of band, read the section of that chapter dealing with how to pull a horse's mane to the desired thickness. Leave the mane a little longer than you would for banding.

Gather your supplies. Shown are yarn the color of the horse's mane, a braiding comb, blunt-nosed scissor, crochet hook (or braid pull), and hairspray (or water).

Wash, or, if the weather is too cold for a traditional bath, spot clean your horse. Do not condition his mane after bathing or the mane will slide right out of your hands as you try to braid. Put a cooler on your horse if it is chilly and he is wet or damp, and put him in cross ties to avoid the post-bath roll. Next,

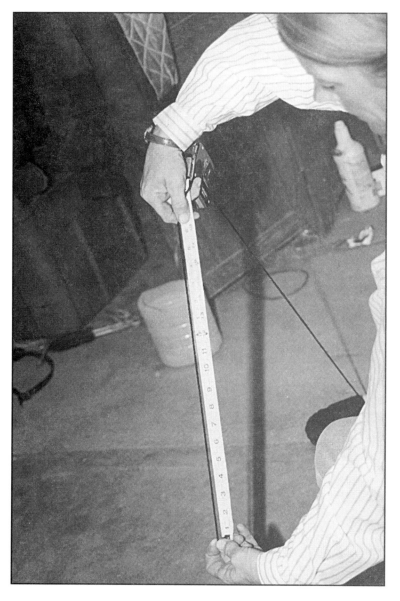

Measure eighteen inches of yarn. A contrasting color was used here for photo purposes.

Before you begin to braid, cut twenty to thirty pieces of the yarn into approximately eighteen-inch lengths.

Stand on a stool if you are too short to reach the top of your horse's mane. Use the braiding comb to section three small, even sections of mane. Use the hair clip to hold the balance of the mane out of your way. Begin to braid those three sections of hair tightly against the base of the horse's neck.

Take one piece of yarn and double it. Halfway down your braid, lay the yarn into the braid. Add one section of the yarn into one segment of the braid; then add the other yarn piece to another segment of braid, leaving the third segment of the hair without a piece of yarn. Continue to braid—incorporating those pieces of yarn into your braid—until you get to the very bottom or end of the braid. Make a knot to keep the end of the braid from unraveling. Try to contain all the loose hairs in the end of the braid.

Insert the braiding pull straight down though the center of the braid at the base of the mane (close the horse's crest). Push it all the way through the braid. Insert the pieces of yarn into the braid pull or hook, and carefully bring the yarn back up through the passageway created by the braid puller. Draw it up until you just see the end of the braid on the knot you made beginning to come through (See photo 8, pg 132). Pull one end of the yarn to each side of the braid. Begin to make a single knot, but before pulling it tight, loop one yarn around the other an additional three to four times. Then pull your knot tight. These additional wraps of the yarn keep it tighter. Tie it with a secure double knot at the

gather the equipment you will need for braiding.

This will include:
• yarn to match your horse's mane
• a braiding comb
• a large hair clip
• a braiding pull or crochet hook
• scissors
• a towel
• a small bucket or spray bottle of water.

base, underneath the braid.

Take the yarn, one piece on either side, and make a loop halfway down the braid. Tie a knot on the top side of the braid. To finish, make another loop, this time ending up under the braid, and make a secure double knot. Cut off the ends of the yarn close to the knot.

Do not cut the loose pieces of hair, because the next time you go to braid, you will find many uneven lengths of hair that will be very hard to contain in a braid. The finished braids should lie flat against the horse's neck; they should not stick up in the air.

Continue down the horse's neck until you have braided the entire mane. Use the yarn to secure and finish each braid, then cut off the ends of the yarn when you have finished. Each braid should be the same size as the previous one. You do not have to use a braiding comb, but it may be helpful. The goal is to have approximately twenty to twenty-five neat little braids down your horse's neck. Although the number may vary from that figure, too few braids will be thick, bulky and unattractive. If the horse has a very long neck, you may need more braids. The number is not important—it is the finished-look that counts. Twenty to twenty-five is just an approximate number to get you started.

Once the horse's mane is neatly braided from top to bottom, put a mane tamer or Slinky on to help hold it down neatly. Watch your horse the first few times so that he does not try to rub the braids out. If you braid the night before a show, check the first thing in the morning to make certain that all the braids stayed in through the night. You

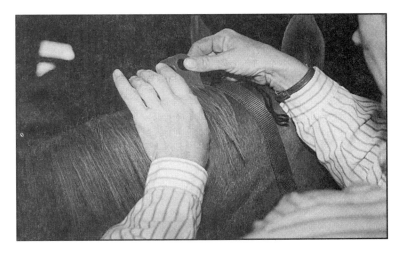

2) Braid the mane as tightly as you can. Close to the horse's neck. Halfway down the length of the braid, lay the yarn into the braid. Place a piece of yarn into two of the three sections of braid.

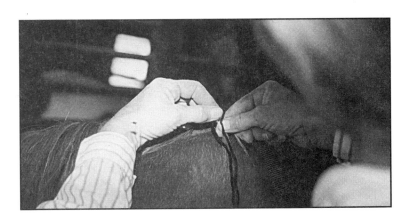

1) Use a braiding comb to get three even sections of hair.

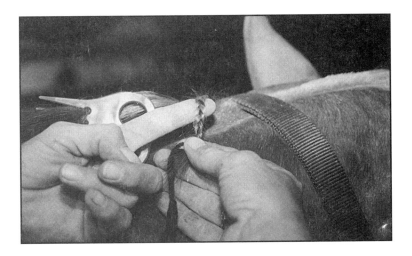

3) Braid the yarn into the mane as shown.

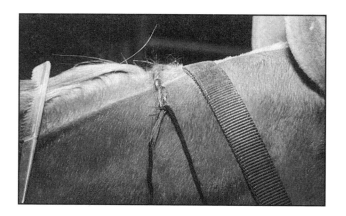

4) *Tie a knot as close to the end as possible.*

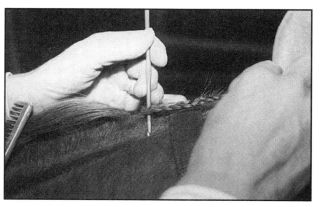

5) *Use a braid pull or a crochet hook to reach through the braid near the crest of the horse's neck.*

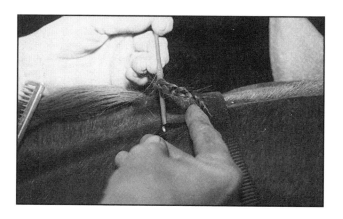

6) *Hook the yarn...*

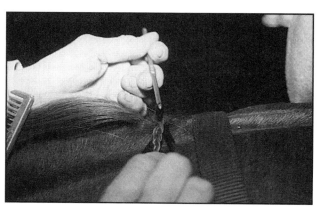

7) *and draw it up through the braid close to the horse's crest...*

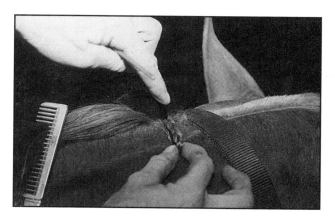

8) *until you just see the end of the braid or the knot that you made beginning to come through.*

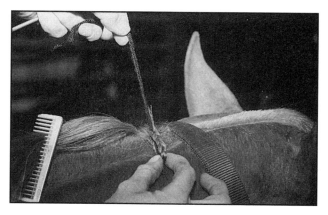

9) *Hold the two tails of yarn and separate them.*

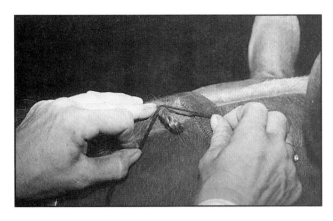

10) Make a single knot, but instead of crossing the yarn once as is normal, make three to four wraps with the yarn in that same single knot.

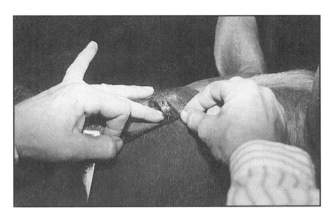

11) Tie the yarn again underneath the braid, and pull it tight to make a knot that won't slip.

12) Bring the ends of your yarn halfway down the braid, still underneath.

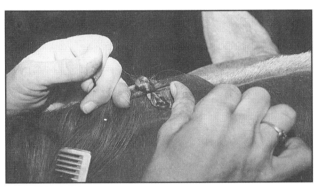

13) Halfway down the braid, make a second knot; leave a small loop in the braided hairs on the top half of your looped braid, and then tie the yarn snugly. The small loop will help make your braid lie flat.

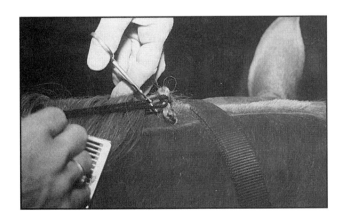

14) Tie another knot under the braid, and cut off the ends of the yarn close to the knot.

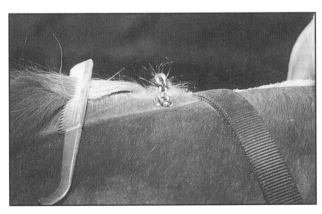

15) Adjust the braid until it is flat against the crest of the horse's neck.

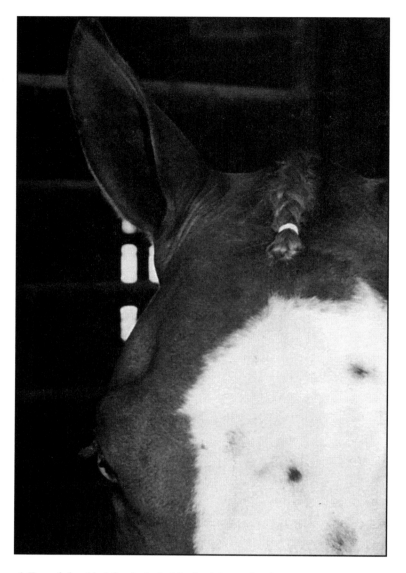

A French braided forelock finished with an elastic.

hairs, start to French braid the forelock. Do this the same way as you do the tail. When you go to cross under with the right section of the forelock, pick up a few hairs with your little finger and add to that section. Cross that section under and add hairs from the other side for the next step in your braid. Alternate adding hairs from the left side and the right side, incorporating them into your braid just as you do for the French braid on the tail.

When you have no more hairs left to pick up, loop yarn around the forelock, just as you did when you added the yarn to the mane braids. Then continue to braid the balance of the forelock. Tie a knot at the end of the braid. Insert the braiding pull from the top of the French braid so that you can pull the entire braid up and underneath the French braid of the forelock. Use your braiding pull to pull the yarn through the top of the braid so that you can tie it once on top and then make a secure double knot on the underside. Tuck the end of the braid under the French-braided segment of the forelock. Cut the ends of the yarn close to the knot. The forelock should now lie flat against the head, giving it a polished, professional look.

BUTTON BRAIDS

Another method of braiding is button braids. To begin, section the hair into twenty or so segments by looping an elastic twice around the hair. The elastic will be loose so that you can easily pull it off each segment of hair as you work. (Save the elastic to contain the ends after you have made the finished braid.) Sectioning the mane first makes the chore quicker and easier.

might have to redo a few, so don't wait until five minutes before your class to check!

Once your horse's mane is braided, proceed to his forelock. The length of the forelock before braiding is about to the middle of his eyes. Take the top third of the forelock and cross the hairs once to begin a braid.

Tip: Comb the forelock and use a comb or your finger to lift the top third of the forelock, closest to his ears, to begin the braid. When you begin the next set of cross-under

Then go back and remove an elastic from one segment and braid the hair of that segment to the end. Put the elastic on the end of the braid. Let the braid hang straight down for now, or until you have braided every section. Then go back and fold the length of the braid either in half or in threes, depending on the length of the finished braid. Use a second elastic to loop around the doubled or tripled braid. You now have a button braid. Finish the entire mane in the same way.

Button braids are quick and easy, although they are not quite as neat as when tied correctly with yarn. Use them for a schooling or open show when you don't want to take the time to use yarn.

No matter which type of braid you choose, the more you practice, the neater your braids will become. Always remove the braids as soon as possible after showing so your horse does not rub and tear out sections of mane.

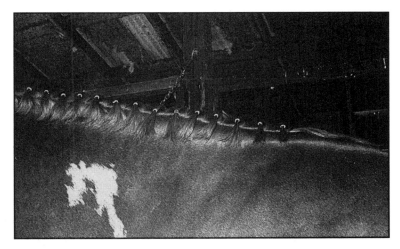

To braid a mane using elastics, first separate the mane and double an elastic to keep the sections apart.

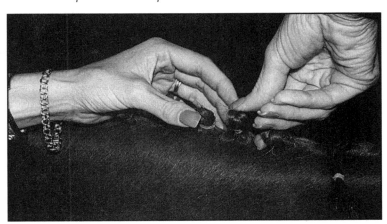

Above: Braid to the end of the hair and put an elastic on it to hold it from unraveling. Then triple the braid going under and use a second elastic to hold it.

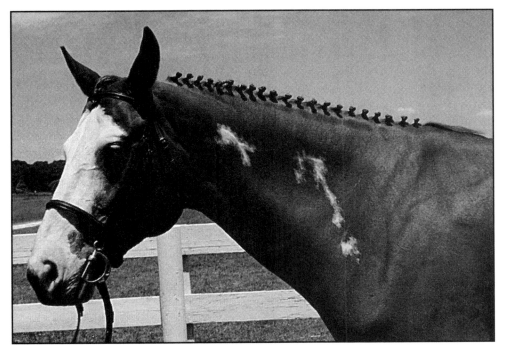

Left: Finished button braids done with elastics.

The finished product, ready for an English showmanship ring, with button braids in the mane, braided forelock, and French braided tail. This is Teddy's Principle, owned by Teresa Grubbs.

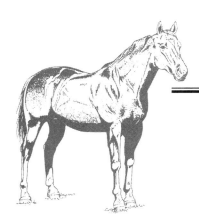

CHAPTER NINETEEN

BRAIDING THE HUNTER'S TAIL

THE FINISHING TOUCH to your hunter's show ring appearance is a nicely braided tail. While this braid may look complicated, with practice it should only take five to ten minutes to complete. You can braid the tail the morning of the show, wrap it with a polo wrap to keep the hairs flat, and unwrap it when you get to the show. Or, as long as your horse doesn't rub his tail, you can braid it the night before the show, cover it with a polo wrap, and undo the wrap at the show.

Beware: Wrapping too tightly will cut off the circulation in his tail. Wrap too loosely and the wrap will fall off. The wrap should be snug—not tight.

While you can wash your horse's tail prior to braiding, *never* put any type of conditioner or glycerine-based product on the tail from the end of the tailbone upward. Otherwise, the hairs, which may be short to begin with near the top of the horse's tail, will slip out of your hand as you braid. You can condition the end of the horse's tail, prior to braiding (from the tip of

the tailbone downward) to give it a silky appearance.

When you are ready to braid the tail, it is preferable to tie your horse in cross ties because it will limit his movement. Apply fly spray *before* you begin so that he will not swish his tail at flies and pull the braid out of your hand. Some horses may get a bit nervous when you stand behind them the first time or two. You might want to practice being behind the horse and handling his tail for a day or two before actually braiding.

Because I can seldom reach the top of the horse's tail, I stand on a stool (or an upturned pail) to start my braid, and step down as I get closer to the end of the braid. This also can make a horse nervous the first time or two. Some horses will wiggle from side to side trying to see what you are doing until they become comfortable with your position. Keep the stool close to the horse so that he has no leverage to hurt you in case he kicks, but let common sense prevail. If your horse is a kicker, you may want to

137

forego braiding his tail. Never put yourself in an unsafe position.

Before you begin to braid, moisten the tail with a wet sponge or towel, or apply a hair gel. This makes it easier to grasp the hairs and keeps them from sliding out of your hand. Then, take three small sections of hair from the top of the horse's tail. The outside two sections, left and right, should be as close to the outside edge of the tailbone as possible. On some horses, the hair in the middle of the horse's tail may be too short to allow you to make the third section of the braid. In this case, form the third section from the edge as well, but as close as you can get to the middle of the tail.

Make one section of a regular braid by crossing the three sections of hair *under*, not over. Crossing the hairs under causes the finished tail to have a neat braid lying down the center of the tail. Crossing the hairs over puts the actual braid underneath so that you don't see the braid running down the center of the tail. (See the accompanying photos—they show both methods.) Be sure to keep the hairs of the braid tight by keeping the braid hairs as close as possible to the tailbone. This will ensure that you have a neat, finished braid at the end, not one that sags.

Cross the first sections of hair once to start your braid as a normal, everyday braid. It starts that way and ends that way, as you will see. Keep the three sections of hair in your fingers held tight to the tail, just as you would when making a normal braid. To start the French braid, take the little finger on your left hand and use it to pick up a fourth, thin section of hair close to the outside of the tailbone on the

left side. (You can also start with hairs on the right side. For ease in explaining, I've chosen to start with the left side.) Bring the section of hair that you just picked up with your little finger and combine it with the section of hair that goes to the middle of your braid—keep putting it under to continue your braid.

Now, pick up another section of hair, this time with the little finger of your right hand. Add this section of hair to the middle section, still going under, not over. Keep working your way down, using your little finger to grasp a section of hair from the outside edge of the horse's tailbone, first on the left side to add to the left section, and then to the right side. Add these thin segments of hair each time you cross under to make a braid.

You will begin to see the braid forming down the center of the horse's tail. Pick up only very tiny sections of hair each time you pick up hair from the edge of the tailbone. Taking too much hair will leave you with a very large braid down the middle of the horse's tail. Tiny sections of hair pulled in from either side make it look neat and tidy. Be sure to keep your braid tight and as close to the tailbone as you can.

When you reach the bottom of the horse's tailbone with your French braid, do not add any more hair to the three sections of hair that you have in your hands. Just use the three sections of hair and make a normal braid about six or eight inches long. Put a braid binder on it so that your entire braid doesn't come undone. Then take the end of your braid where the braid binder is and make a loop. Loop your long braid underneath and put another binder there, close to the bottom of your French braid. Tuck the loose hairs on the end of this small braid up under the French braid. Hold your hand at the end of the braid and carefully brush the horse's tail so that any loose hairs will blend in with the balance of the tail.

Slightly dampen the entire braid, from the top of the tail to the bottom loop. Then carefully wrap it with a polo wrap, starting at the top and working your way down. This will help the hair to stay flat. Don't wrap so tightly that it will cut off the circulation in the horse's tail, but it must not be so loose that it will slide off if the horse swishes his tail.

You may want to practice a time or two, starting lower on the horse's tail where the hairs are a bit longer and therefore much easier to work with. Once you've practiced on the longer hairs, then begin your braid at the top of the tailbone. The first inch or two of braiding is always the hardest because the hairs are so short. For this reason, take extra care of your horse's tail, and be sure to immediately correct any signs of tail rubbing.

Condition your horse's tail on the days following a show (never right before you plan to braid the tail), and add extra conditioner to the top or base of his tail to encourage the hair to grow. Condition your horse's tail hairs every time you hose or wash him, and leave the conditioner in. Do not rinse it out.

When you're finished showing for the day, remove the first braid binder, pull the long braid out so that you can remove the second binder, and, *using only your fingers*, gently unbraid the tail and brush it out.

Both braiding and wrapping will become easier with time, since practice makes perfect. The accompanying photos will help you to visualize the steps involved.

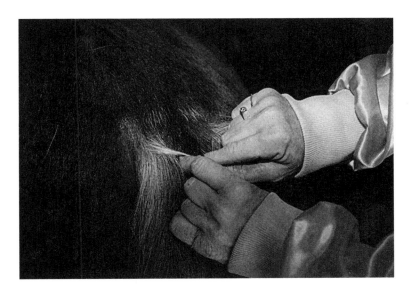

1) Take three sections of hair from the top of the horse's tail. The two outside sections, left and right, should be as close to the outside as possible—the middle from wherever you can get enough hair.

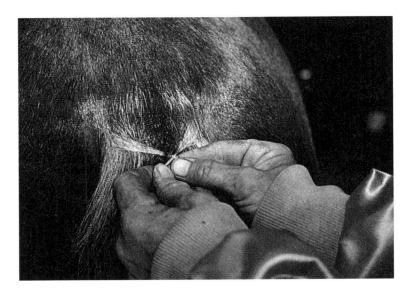

2) Start by making one section of a braid. Cross the hairs under, not over, to create the little braid on the top that lies down the length of the larger braid. Be sure to keep the braid tight and as close to the tail bone as possible. This will present a neat, finished braid.

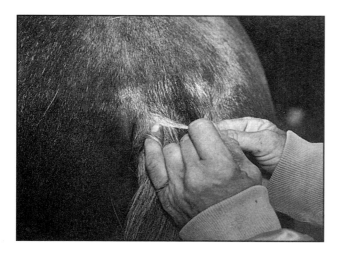

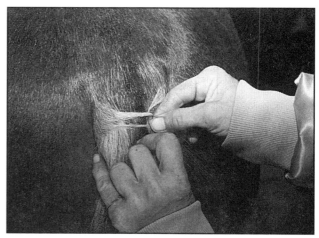

3) Keep the three sections of hair in your fingers just as you would when making a normal braid. Take your little finger and use it to pick up a fourth, thin section of hair, again from close to the outside of the tailbone. I'm picking up a very small section of hair—just a few hairs—from the left side of the tailbone in this photo.

4) Bring the section of hair that you just picked up and combine it with the next section that you put under to make the next segment of your braid.

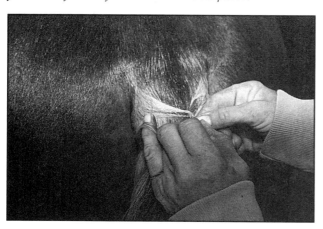

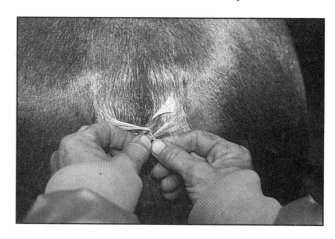

5) Keep working your way down, using your little finger to grasp a small section of hair from the very outside edge of the horse's tailbone...

6) ...first on the left side to add to the left section that will go underneath...

7) ...and then on the right side.

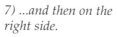

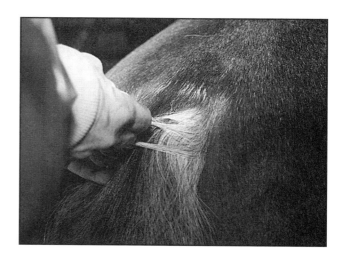

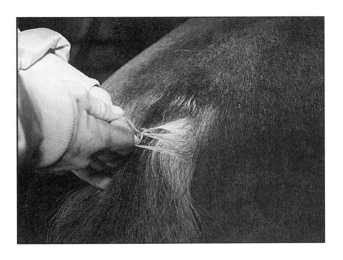

8) Add these thin segments of hair each time that you cross under to make a section of braid.

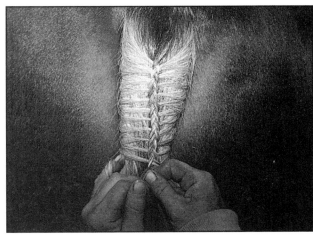

9) You will begin to see the braid forming down the center of the horse's tail.

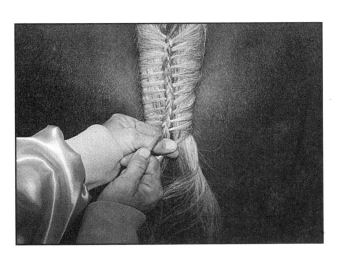

10) Add to a section of hair, cross under to braid.

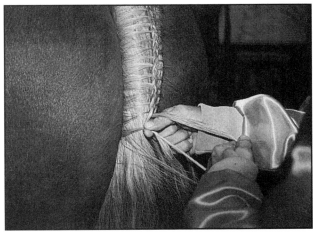

11) To keep the braid tight and close to the tailbone, when you pick up the added section of hair, grasp the hairs to add to your existing section of braid a little off center so that as you braid it pulls the braid tight. As you add hairs from each side, the braid will stay centered and tight. If this confuses you, first perfect your braiding technique, and then come back and read this caption. It is not absolutely necessary, but it is one of those tricks that helps to keep your braid tight and close to the tailbone.

12) When you reach the bottom of the tail bone, do not add any more hairs from the side of the tail to the three sections that you have in your hand.

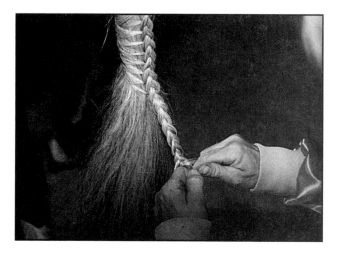

13) Just continue making a normal braid about seven to eight inches long.

14) Put a braid binder on the end of that braid so it can not come undone.

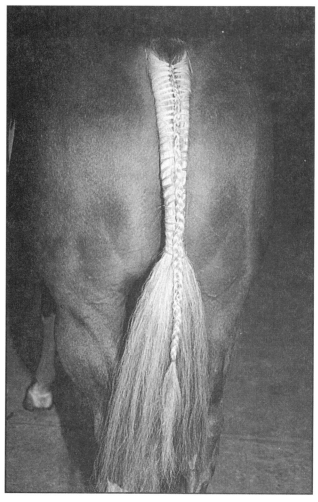

15) Here is how the tail looks so far. Don't stop yet!

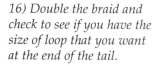

16) Double the braid and check to see if you have the size of loop that you want at the end of the tail.

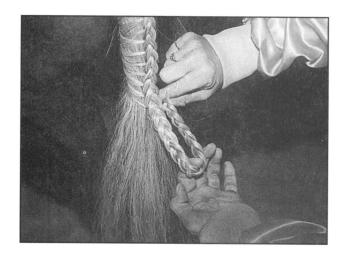

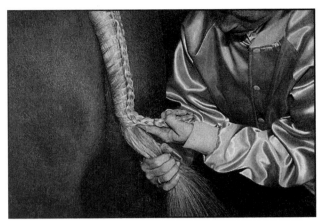

17) Then take hold of the end of the braid, where the braid binder is, and form a loop that goes underneath. Put another binder here, close to the end of your French braid.

18) Tuck the loose hairs up and under the French braid. Then hold the bottom of the French braid and carefully brush the end of the horse's tail. You can wrap the entire tail overnight. That will help to keep the hairs flat and will protect the braid overnight.

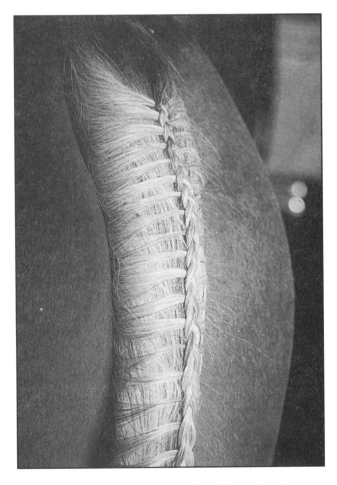

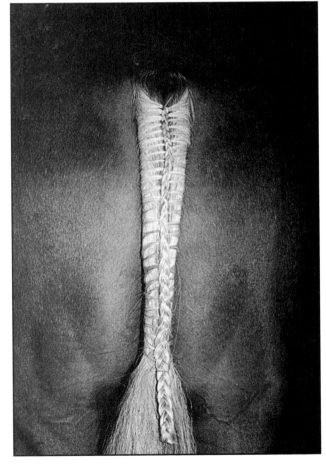

19) Here you can see a nice, neat braid running down the center of the tail.

20) The finished tail.

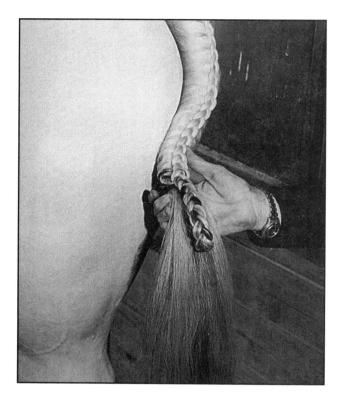

The colors of this Paint mare's tail make a very interesting braid.

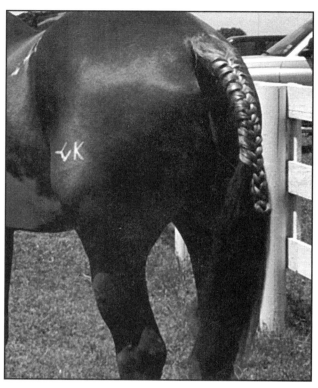

Braiding the hairs over, rather than under, will give you this look.

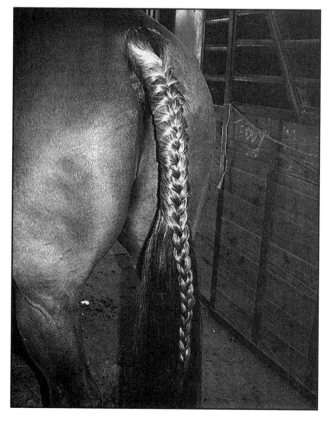

1) You can braid to the end of the hairs and...

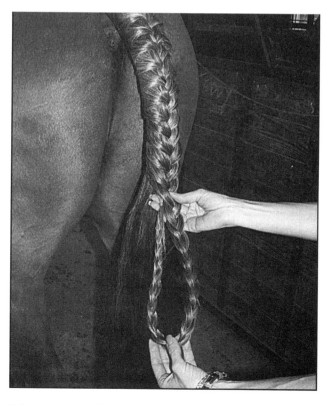

2) loop once and then...

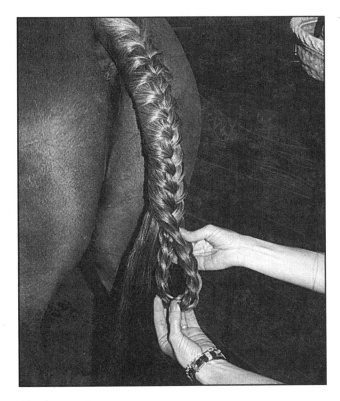

3) ...loop twice...

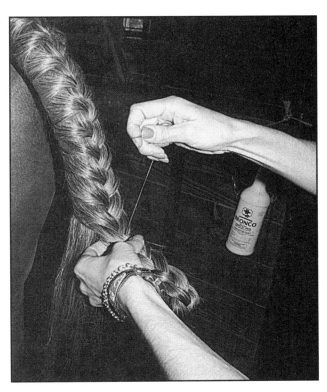

4) ...and sew it to fasten it.

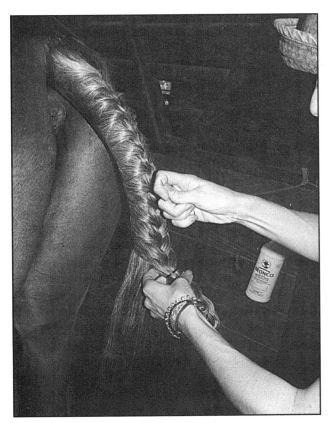

5) Use a strong rug thread and make a couple of loops to hold it.

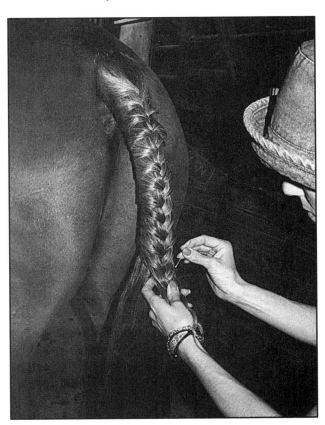

6) Tie it off underneath. Using thread that matches the color as the tail hides any evidence of fastening the braid.

CHAPTER TWENTY

HOW SHOWMANSHIP CLASSES ARE SCORED

YOUR HORSE is clipped, braided or banded, and groomed to perfection. He knows the showmanship maneuvers and performs them without fail. You've found clothes that you feel good in and that match your horse. Your halter and lead line are spotless, and your silver is gleaming down to the very last buckle. You're ready to make your showmanship debut after spending hours and hours practicing. But do you know the rules for the class or how it is judged and scored?

The American Quarter Horse Association rules use a score of zero to twenty, in half-point increments. Ten of those points are gained through the horse's performance, while the remaining ten are based on the overall appearance of the horse and exhibitor.

The overall appearance of horse and handler are judged on items such as appropriate attire—either English or western—your confidence and manner, and your ability to present your horse. You must stand upright and avoid unnatural or exaggerated body positions. You must "show" the horse throughout the entire class.

Ready to load up for a show.

Stand up tall and be proud of the horse that you show. Attitude counts!

147

Never lose sight of the fact that this class started as a way to show a halter horse. Therefore, you must present your horse in his best light. Your *manner* of showing—i.e., being poised and confident—is judged, as is your *ability* to present the horse properly. Also included in these ten points are the horse's body condition or fitness, his clipping, banding and braiding, and overall grooming. The horse must be clean and conditioned, with mane and tail free from tangles, and his hoofs must be properly shod or trimmed.

The other ten points are based on performance. Patterns must be worked accurately and precisely. The horse must obey you with a minimum of cues and must be obedient to your every command. Knocking over a cone, working on the wrong side of a cone, and not following the pattern exactly as it is written are penalized severely.

Faults can be minor, major, or severe. A minor fault will cost you from one-half to four points. A major fault will cost four and one-half points *and up* off your score. To quote from the Quarter Horse rule book:

Out of condition.

In condition.

Faults of the overall appearance of the horse or exhibitor can include, but are not limited to:

- Poorly groomed, conditioned, or trimmed horse.
- Dirty, ragged, or ill-fitting halter or lead.
- Poor or improper position of the exhibitor.
- Excessively stiff, artificial, or unnatural movements around the horse or when leading.
- Changing hands on the lead line.

Faults of the performance include:
- Drifting of horse when being led—in other words, the horse not traveling in a straight line.
- Horse stopping crooked or cocking or resting one hip.
- Excessive amount of time required to set the horse up.
- Failure to perform the maneuver at the marker.

Severe faults include:
- Leading on the right side of the horse.
- Touching the horse or hand placing his feet.
- Obstructing the judge's view of the horse.
- Omission or addition of maneuvers.
- Knocking over a cone.
- Rearing, pawing, or kicking other horses in the arena.

Disqualification:
- Willful abuse.
- Loss of control of the horse.
- Failure to wear a number in a visible spot.
- Excessive schooling.

The following rules are taken from the American Paint Horse rule book:

While the horse or his conformation is not judged, the horse's appearance (i.e. hair coat, grooming, conditioning, trimming, and tack), is 40 percent of your total score. The breakdown of that 40 percent is as follows:
- Condition and thriftiness— 15 points.
- Grooming—the hair coat clean with mane and tail free of tangles and hooves properly trimmed or shod—15 points.
- Trimming of the mane, face and lower leg hairs—5 points.
- The cleanliness and condition of your halter and lead line—5 points.

If you pull a horse out of the pasture with a shaggy coat and unclipped mane, or in a poor or thin condition, you will lose forty points just by walking into the arena with an unprepared horse. Of that forty, fifteen points are based on condition and thriftiness. The horse should be in good condition, neither too fat nor too thin. An underweight, undernourished horse screams for a better feeding program and most judges find that offensive. A horse that is too fat tells a judge that this horse has not been in a proper conditioning program. All the grooming in the world cannot hide the fact that you have not conditioned him. A conditioned horse is a healthy horse. His muscling is attractive and gives him an overall bloom that shouts, "Look at me!"

Fifteen points are given to a horse that has a clean hair coat and is well groomed. That means the grass stains on his hocks and on his white legs (or spots if he is a Paint) must go. French White® chalk, baby powder, or even corn starch will help to brighten up white areas, and is handy to have in your grooming box. If you apply a good coating of Show Sheen® the night before a show after bathing the horse, you can usually brush the dirt off his coat the next morning without having to give him an actual bath. His mane and tail should be well brushed. Knots and burrs in his mane or tail show that you do not care about this class nor about how your horse looks.

YOUR APPEARANCE

Your appearance is 10 percent of the total score. You must wear suitable clothing that is neat and clean and appropriate for the time of year and type of show. A registered breed show requires that you dress according to their standards. The neatness and cleanliness of your attire are being judged. In other words, do not enter the ring with the pants and boots that you gave your horse a bath or cleaned his stall in. Your appearance just helps to make a better overall picture in the riding classes, but in showmanship it is given an actual numerical score.

SHOWING YOUR HORSE

Showing your horse in the ring—performing the various ma-neuvers following a predescribed pattern—is 50 percent of your total score.

Of that 50 percent:
- Leading the horse properly—15 points.
- Posing your horse properly—15 points.
- Your poise and ability to show your horse to the best of your ability—20 points.

Following the pattern *exactly* as it is written will obviously increase your score for that 50-percent segment of the class. Many hours must be spent at home, both training and conditioning prior to showing, if you want to increase your odds of success.

SHOWING ENGLISH

If you are showing in an English hunt-seat class, you must have the mandatory breeches or jodhpurs in either buff, gray, rust, or canary. Tall boots are required for adults, and jodhpur boots are acceptable for children. Both adults and children must wear a fitted jacket with a choker and stock pin and a hard hat or safety helmet. The same rules apply, except that you show an English horse in a bridle, most often a snaffle. Your horse should be braided, not banded, with mane, tail, and forelock all braided neatly.

READ YOUR RULES

Looking at the above list of rules gives you some quick and easy pointers—ways to increase your points, or ways to *lose points* if you haven't read your rule book carefully. English or western, your "job" as a showmanship handler is to make the horse that you are leading look good. Remember to keep

With a well-groomed, well-trained horse, those once elusive showmanship ribbons should begin to head your way. Good luck!

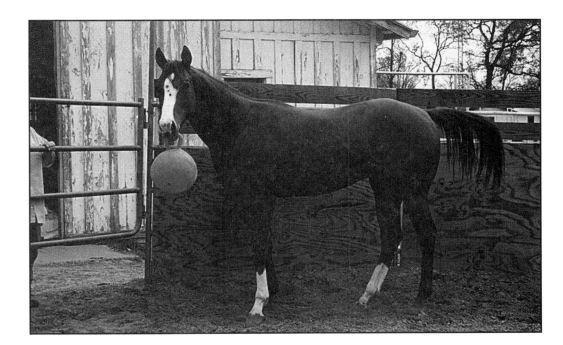

*Don't forget!
Even a
showmanship
horse needs play
time!*

your attention focused. Watch the judge, but glance frequently at the horse so that at all times you will know his position. Never obstruct the judge's view of the horse; you must switch from side to side as he does. Even as he prepares to pin the class, the judge will often glance at the competitors to be sure that they are continuing to show their horses. Your presentation is never over until the ribbons are handed out. More than once a judge has changed his placings at the last minute.

Have fun showing, whether you win or lose, and don't take it too seriously! Learn from your mistakes and from observing successful exhibitors at the larger shows. And remember to keep it fun for your horse, too.

Happy showing!

The author, without a horse!

Left to right: Sons Jon and Don Truskauskas, Dan Delaney, and Don Bunn, Jr., after winning a race in the author's truck.

It's never too early to start training! The author's grandson, Micheal.

ABOUT THE AUTHOR

Laurie C. Truskauskas was born in Bristol, Connecticut, and began riding at the age of three. She learned to train Quarter Horses while working as an apprentice to Joe Ferro, reining trainer and one of the founding members of the American Quarter Horse Association. Later, she trained horses on her own for a number of years in Connecticut before moving to Texas in 1997.

Here, she fulfilled a lifelong dream—owning a beautiful horse farm where the weather is suitable for training horses year-round. The move proved to be the right one. With three breeding stallions, horses in training, numerous lessons, and boarding, Silver Creek Farm is active continuously. Truskauskas starts colts, retrains older horses, shows horses, and has many young students learning to jump low fences, opening up the world of jumping and English riding to the children of Athens, Texas, and surrounding areas.

Truskauskas began the long process of learning to write when a neck operation made her realize that the day could come when she wouldn't be able to climb on the back of another horse. She began writing for numerous periodicals in 1994. In addition to this book, she has published *Training the Two-Year-Old Colt*, and is looking forward to the publication of two additonal titles: one on training the western horse and one on schooling for trail class obstacles and patterns.

By putting on paper the knowledge she has gained from training, Truskauskas hopes that she can help more people to enjoy a life filled with horses.

YOU'LL WANT TO READ THESE, TOO . . .

The ABC's of Showmanship
Teach the Showmanship Maneuvers Step by Step
Laurie Truskauskas
Pocket-sized companion to this book gives concise instructions on patterns and showmanship exercises.
An Alpine Arena Handbook
Comb binding, ISBN 1-57779-631-6

Horse Anatomy, A Coloring Atlas
Robert Kainer, DVM and Thomas McCracken, MS
This unique learning tool has eighty-one detailed drawings of all parts of the horse accompanied by descriptions and common problems affecting that portion of the anatomy. The reader is invited to color in as you read to enjoy an almost "hands-on" experience. Selected as reference material for National 4-H Horse Bowl and Hippology competition.
Wire bound, Softcover ISBN 1-57779-017-0

Illustrated Dictionary of Equine Terms
New Horizon Equine Learning Center
Over 300 pages of definitions covering everything from training and medical terms to breeds and equipment. An excellent reference for anyone working with horses or horse subject matter.
Hardcover, ISBN 0-931866-88-X
Softcover, ISBN 1-57779-014-6

Mental Equitation
James Arrigon
The first book to provide a proven, systematic program of riding based on the theories of classical horsemanship. Equally applicable for western and English riders. The author is a University equitation instructor and coach of a successful collegiate equestrian team.
Hardcover, ISBN 1-57779-010-3

Almost a Whisper
Sam Powell
Learn to communicate effectively and safely with your horse and how his instincts as a herd and a prey animal affect how you should handle and train him. Powell is a master horseman and shares his years of experience and observation in a manner anyone can understand and use. Covers colt starting, trailer loading, problem solving and more.
Hardcover, ISBN 1-57779-026-X

Training the Two-Year-Old Colt
Laurie Truskauskas
With this book as your guide you can start your first horse with confidence. Start by teaching your weanling basic manners and continue step by step through your two-year-old's first thirty days under saddle and beyond. Truskauskas is a trainer and exhibitor of western pleasure and reining horses who learned her trade under the skillful guidance of trainer Joe Ferro of Quarter Horse fame.
Hardcover, ISBN 1-57779-004-9

How to Use Leg Wraps, Bandages & Boots
Sue A. Allen
The only book to explain all types of wraps, boots and bandages, and how and when to use them. Also covers preventative care and treatment for leg injuries and strains. Allen is a riding instructor and often gives clinics on equine leg care.
Softcover, ISBN 0-931866-72-3

COMING SOON BY THE SAME AUTHOR:
Training the Junior Trail Horse
Training the Western Horse

These and other fine Alpine titles are available at your local bookseller or you may order direct from the publisher at 1-800-777-7257 or writing to Alpine Publications, 225 S. Madison Ave., Loveland, CO 80537.

For the latest information and prices check our website: www.AlpinePub.com.